Dear Kathy
Happy Baking
God bless your
hands as your
prepare and keep
your healthy
Love
2P

766 - 0472

2P's Treasures Cook Book

2P's Treasures Cook Book

From My Kitchen to Your Kitchen

No Sugar, No Dairy Made with Spelt
For Allergies, Candida and Diabetes

First Published by Jeannine Edwards 2006
Second Published by Friends Publishing, Inc. 2006
Health & Cooking

ISBN: 0-9788615-5-8   Trade Paperback

Printed in the United States of America

This book is printed on acid-free paper.

Friends Publishing, Inc.
www.FriendsPublishing.com

2P's Treasures Cook Book
From My Kitchen to Your Kitchen

No Sugar, No Dairy Made with Spelt
For Allergies, Candida and Diabetes

By

Jeannine '2P'　　　Edwards

TABLE OF CONTENTS

Author & Restaurant Owner
Jeannine '2P' Edwards

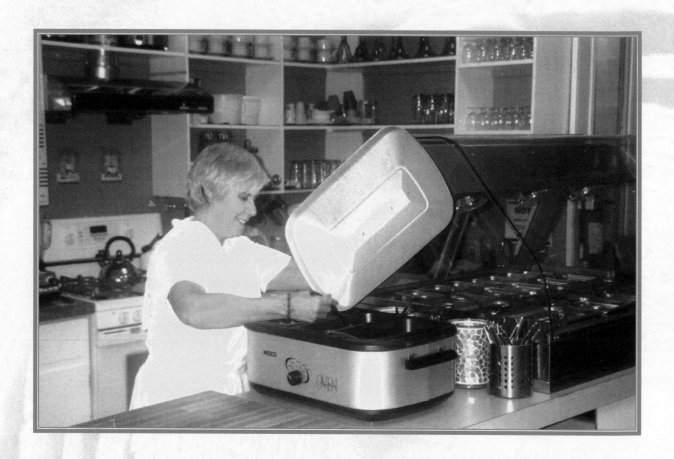

Welcome to my Kitchen!

Preface

2P's Health Kitchen Restaurant in Vernon, B.C., Canada (Simulcast B.C. Television) cooks for her community from these tasty recipe treasures. This Cook Book will save your life! 2P's Treasures is filled with "Inulin" producing foods and recipes for your health. You can have flavor and sweets the healthy way. Enjoy!

From My Kitchen to Your Kitchen,
With Love, 2P Edwards

~God's Blessings~

2P's Health Kitchen Restaurant
Vernon, B.C. Canada

Introduction

These recipes have been my treasures as they have helped me survive because of allergies and other health issues. In this age of fast foods and busy people, we don't have the time to cook the way Gramma did, so we range into fast food places or pick up packaged foods on the shelves of our grocery stores and we eat these foods to sustain us. We all do it.

Unfortunately, when we start to look into what is entering our bodies (which were actually lent to us) we sometimes, too late realize the damage we have done ourselves. How can we possibly digest all those additives and preservatives? We are on a fast train of destruction. How do we slow it down? What about our children? We have to start somewhere and this is what I have done. I now eat according to what my body can digest or take. What about you? Would you consider going to a Naturopathic Doctor, have yourself checked to see what allergies you have and start following a healthy diet of foods you can digest?

I am now 67 and so far not on any medications. I take treatment from Dr. Wagstaff whenever I am not doing well and that happens when I break my diet. It's when I go shopping and can't find a place to eat most times. There is wheat, dairy and sugar in everything. When I go out socially I cannot eat, and when I do, I suffer the consequences. We have to take charge of our own health. We have to be responsible for ourselves. Please don't wait until it is too late.

There are so many auto- immune diseases out there, more than ever before and it has gone rampant. For your sake and for the sake of your precious body, takes the time to look into what you are feeding your family and yourself. Take time to adjust to foods that are good for you. We are so used to eating heavy meals, junk and sweet desserts. We need more fresh organic vegetables and fruit. Unless you have Candida, then you must be careful about your intake of anything yeast or sugar producing.

I was going to make up a book on cheeses and decided that Tofu, Nutritional Yeast and nuts would be used. This is not recommended for Candida sufferers. I use goat feta sometimes and always check when I order Greek Salad as not all places use goat but often use the dairy feta.

I buy the soy cheese on rare occasions. I like to use it on pizza and sometimes add it to a cream sauce. I encourage you to use all the healthiest of ingredients. The water should be purified, lemons organic and sea salt is best. Coconut oil is excellent! So is grapeseed oil. I found a new shortening by Earth Balance and it makes wonderful pie crust and cookies. You will find it in your Health Food Store or check it out on line.

The best of 2P's Recipe Collection #1 and Collection #2.

Collection #1 consists of the following:

- Bonus Book
- Cream Soup Solutions
- Bread Bin
- Cream Sauce Solutions

- Cool Cakes & Frostings
- Plentiful Pies
- Cookies & Squares

Collection #2 consists of the following:

- Bonus Book
- Mighty Muffins
- Jams, Jellies & Gelatins

- Dessert by Dezine
- Pancakes/Crepes
- Pasta/Rice

This book contains recipes found in 2P's Recipe Cook Book Collection's #1 and #2

2p's Treasures? What does it mean?

First you may say **"2p"**. What does it mean? Well it was the name given to me at the age of 9 months when I began to walk. My **Memere (Grandmother)** named me **"Toupie"** meaning a **"Spinning Top"** in the **French language** and the **"nick name"** stuck.

For many years, I struggled with my poor health, and I tried everything to alter my diet on a daily basis so I could feel somewhat normal again. It was these recipes that kept me fed. They became my treasures. I pray that they will become yours, and optimally you will not feel the deprivation of great tasting food from any allergies/dietary restrictions or health conditions. Cook, bake and enjoy these recipes! It took me years to find a way to bring this knowledge of learning to combine, cook research and feed myself these healthy food recipes. I bring you this cook book because I want to share them with you.

I pray that this will be helpful,

Jeannine '2p' Edwards

Acknowledgments

I have so many to thank. I will start by thanking you personally for buying my book. It is such an encouragement. I am especially grateful for a loving God who answers prayer. For Dr. Craig Wagstaff, N.D, from Healthtrek Research Inc. For his treatments and his wonderful staff who have been a source of encouragement, guidance and help for years and have been a haven for me in my time of need. My husband Chuck, who has spent money and time helping me regain my health and putting up with all the eating experiments and never complaining.

Many thanks for my good friend GG (98 years young) who is daring, uplifting and game, and who gives me sound advice. For Michael, my son, David my grandson who dared to eat everything I made. For all my children, who don't hold it against me for passing on all these allergies. For my daughter, Debbie LaFramboise, who has been my rock. For Chef Lawrence my son whose support has been appreciated. He shares the love of cooking with me. Thankful for, my grandchildren Jerry and Jessika LaFramboise and twins Ashley and Breanna Gionette that have eaten my baking. They enjoy everything put before them.

Thanks to my friends, Gloria Jackson and Ann Kibblewhite who have been so helpful. Danica Lloyd, Vernon Vitamin Center, has been a strong support to my cause. Graeme Osborn, Wayside Press, for the sign and all his patience, work and printing. A big thank you to OK Color Lazer for all the late work on my small cookie book. Last and not least Julie & Grant from Simply Delicious (my home away from home) that have been so encouraging and supportive. They have allowed me to demo, sell my products as well as the books. The staff has been wonderful. Nile at Nature's Fare has always been sweet and helpful and always made me feel welcome. To Terry from Nature's Fare in Kelowna and her staff. God Bless you all. I am so blessed to have all these wonderful people in my life. Lori-Ann Baron for her encouragement. It's good to have kids that are supportive. Vivian Cochrane has been a great help also. She has tried a lot of the recipes as I was making them. I just love her as a sister.

I am so grateful to those who have been active in playing a part in the opening of my restaurant, 2p's Heath Kitchen. Special thanks to Peter Lockhart of Royal LePage. I am planning to help those with afflictions such as allergies, candida, celiac, diabetes and have vegetarian, raw and vegan food as well as organic. I will have some organic chicken, turkey, buffalo and wild fish at 2P's Health Kitchen restaurant to cater to everyone's palate. I never thought writing these books would lead to this. What a fulfilling life it has become for myself and my husband Chuck. Thank you for reading, and we hope you will enjoy 2P's Treasures Cook Book!

Much Love, Jeannine '2P' Edwards

Spelt

Spelt flour is an ancient grain mentioned in the Bible. It is not tampered with like regular wheat. It comes in 2 different forms. I use the organic light. It is lighter than the brown or whole spelt. Many with wheat allergies can tolerate it but it is wiser to have this checked out by a ND. It is high in gluten.

For those who can tolerate spelt, you will find it is dryer than wheat. It is high in B1, B2, and B17, which support the body's cancer fighting mechanism. It is the only grain that contains mucopolysaccharides, which stimulates the immune system. It is high in carbohydrates, contains more crude fiber and protein than wheat including all the amino acids.

It is wonderful in pastries, breads, muffins, cakes, cookies, gravies, sauces, coatings and all pertaining to flour. It is more costly than regular flour but the benefits are worth it.

Chicolin®

For Candida it stimulates bifid bacteria growth in the intestine. Stimulates the immune system and aids the absorption of B vitamins. It derives from the chicory plant.

Inulin is its major component (87% of the powder weight). It is a soluble fiber.

(1) Low glycemic index does not stimulate insulin secretion.
(2) Non-digestible plant sugars. It passes through the digestive system unchanged.
(3) Contains l molecular weight sugar Oligosaccharides.
(4) Slows the absorption of sugars until it reaches the large intestine, are not digested in the upper gastrointestinal tract. Fortifies foods with fiber in the colon.
(5) Regulates blood sugar, does not lead to a rise in serum.

Inulin Producing Foods

For those who have Diabetes, this is a very important section in the book for you to read. If you add these food groups to your diet on a regular basis, your digestive tract will produce natural insulin in the form of "inulin" – that which is naturally made after eating these foods; Artichokes (or anything in the sunflower/artichoke family), Green Beans and Blueberries. Blueberry pie, steamed artichokes and steamed green beans are just a few simple additions to your diet when you need to get your blood sugar levels and diabetes under control.

(1) Does produce and stimulate "inulin" (natural insulin) secretion.
(2) Regulates blood sugar, does not lead to a rise in serum.

Here is a list of "inulin" producing foods that you can find at most any health food or Co-op store;

blueberries, artichokes, green beans, bitter melon (green squash), fenugreek (the spice), stevia, sunflower root family (burdock, chickory, dandelion), onions, garlic, scallions, leeks and pine nuts.

Stevia

Stevia is an herb whose leaves are 300 times sweeter than sugar. It will tell you that you may mix 1 container of each. This will be a sweet mixture. I have experimented with it for 3 years and I have found a combination that works here for us, as I do not fancy the taste of stevia. I think that we should all use it as we feel is right. Some like very sweet, as others prefer it not so sweet. I had to adjust it for my family, so I use 1 container of 250 grams of Chicolin® and 2½ teaspoons of stevia shaking the container every time I use it. It works well for me. You may mix it according to your taste. We have had a hard time finding the Stevina™ brand. I have tried many stevias but the one I find acceptable is Now Stevia.

3 Tablespoons = 1 cup sugar,
*This is not written in stone.
Experiment!

Dairy

Dairy is omitted in my recipes but the recipes allow you to use the milk of your choice for baking and cooking.

In Alive Magazine #132 July/August 1993 Page 8, Dr. Joseph Campbell Ph. D, quotes," The Chinese drink no milk, average half as much calcium as we do, yet have very little osteoporosis. They consume one third less protein, most of which comes from plant sources." He goes on to say, "We are the only species that drink the milk of another species, yet it is the most allergenic food on earth."

I use a little goat's milk in some of the recipes to enrich the sauces, and in other recipes I use rice milk. All of these recipes are changeable and adaptable depending on what you can use. As for milk there are numerous milks made from grain, seed or nut. Soy milk or Rice Dream are some of the non-dairy milks available by example.

In making seed or nut milk the measure is usually 1cup seeds or nuts to 2 cups of purified water in the blender until it is liquefied. You may sweeten it with a pinch of Chicolin®/stevia and 1 tsp. vanilla or leave plain for cooking.

I prefer sunflower seeds and cashews. Sesame seed is very high in protein and it also can be used. I use raw peanuts if the Candida is under control, so it depends on what you are able to tolerate. My suggestion is to go easy on yourself and focus on these healthful recipes as a new culinary adventure! Not a battle.

What About Fat?

In this Collection I try to keep the fat at a minimum although we do need fat in our diets. Knowing which fat raises or helps lower Cholesterol is extremely important.

Saturated fats raise cholesterol and should be limited. Most come from animal or plant such as palm oil. The hydrogenated fats also are very undesirable. This is in the form of margarine and shortening and is acceptable if they contain no more than 2 grams of fat per tablespoon. It should be marked on the label. Polyunsaturated fats and monounsaturated fats are from plants. Poly is safflower, sesame and sesame seed, corn and soybean, nuts and seeds and their oils. Mono is Canola, olive, peanut and avocado. These may help lower your cholesterol. A moderate intake of all oils is best. Earth Balance shortening has become my favorite for pies and is zero (0%) cholesterol.

Omega Nutrition Coconut Oil, which is 100% organic and is not hydrogenated, contains no trace of *Trans fatty acids,* perfect for vegans and is dairy free. There are 2 groups of saturated fats -medium and long chain. This information is taken from Carl Levin, Executor Director of the US Council and handed out with the Coconut oil information. It states that Coconut oil is lower in calories, valuable to those who have trouble digesting fats, and contains Lauric Acid. You may use less to obtain the same results in your recipes as found in the brochure.

I received e-mail from Dr. Alex Sevanian with information on Grape Seed oil. He states that the content of saturated fat is low the content percentage contains most polyunsaturated fats (up to 70%) followed by Monounsaturated fat, and then about 7% saturated fats. He says that natural oils contain some saturated fats for various nutritional and metabolic needs. Grape seed has a lot of linoleic acid, the main form of polyunsaturated fats. I thought that was very nice of Dr. Sevanian to personally give me this information.

Earth Balance products are also wonderful. I use both the Shortening and the Butter. It makes light flaky pastry and the butter is excellent for cookies and cakes.

Recipes for the Basics

Homemade Baking Powder

½ cup cream of tartar
¼ cup arrowroot powder **or** tapioca
¼ cup baking soda

Mix well and keep dry. Makes 1 cup. Always use even soda and arrowroot or tapioca to twice the cream of tartar. Good for celiacs.

Egg Replacement

You may buy egg replacer at your health food store. I have used it and it is good. I use the Flaxseed Gel as well.

Flaxseed Gel

2½ cups purified water
7 Tbsp. organic flaxseed

In a small pot, bring the water to a boil. Add the flaxseed. Remove from the stove and strain all at once. It thickens really fast. Cool and keep in the refrigerator. ¼ cup of flaxseed =1 egg. You can use crushed flaxseed (grounded in a coffee grinder and not bother to strain it). They both work well.

Cold Method of Flaxseed Gel

3 cups flaxseed
1 cup purified water

Grind the flaxseed in the blender; add the water blend until thick. 3 Tbsp. =1 egg. Can be frozen in 1 egg or 2 egg portions.

Better Butter

1 pound butter
1 cup Udo or Flaxseed oil

Beat together until creamy. Place in small containers and keep cool.

💡 This is good for bread, toast, veggies, etc.
Not for cooking.

Better Butter #2

1 pound butter
1 cup grapeseed oil

Blend and cream together Good for cooking as well as a spread for bread and toast. Use where butter is needed.

Cream Soup Solution Collection

These soups speak for themselves. You will find recipes for soups that have the taste and texture of creamed soups for those who cannot tolerate dairy. There is cream of cauliflower, potato, broccoli, carrot, mushroom, celery and chicken. You will find recipes to make canned cream soups as well so that you can use them in your entrée recipes when called for instead of commercial canned soups. Instead of spelt flour, potato flour can be used for celiac as we do in the restaurant. Remember when a hot bowl of cream tomato soup was out of the question on a chilly night. Even in the heat of the day, a cold bowl of chilled cucumber soup was refreshing but you had to forgo because you are unable to have dairy.

Cream of Turnip Soup

1 cup peeled, diced and washed potatoes
1¼ cup diced white turnip
1 diced onion
2 Tbsp. each Better Butter and spelt flour (celiac–use potato flour)
6 cups vegetable **or** chicken broth
1 cup favorite milk (rice, soy, seed, nut or goat)

Place the potatoes, turnip and onions in butter in pan and cook for 10 minutes. Add the broth and simmer until veggies are cooked. Place half in the blender and blend until creamy. Return to pan and add the milk. Serve hot.

Cauliflower Soup A La Crème

2 Tbsp. coconut oil **or** grapeseed oil
1 medium diced onion
6 cups vegetable **or** chicken broth
1 level tsp. onion powder
½ tsp. garlic powder
1½ Tbsp. dried **or** 3 Tbsp. fresh parsley flakes
¾ cup grated celery
2½ cups grated potatoes
2/3 cup grated carrots
2 cups favorite milk (I do 1 goat and 1 rice but it's your choice)
2 cups chopped cauliflower

In a large pot, cook onion in oil. Add the next 7 ingredients and cook until vegetables are soft. Add milk and do not boil. Add the cauliflower Simmer 20 minutes until cauliflower is soft. Cream 1/3 of the soup in the blender, return to the pot with the rest of the soup.

To make canned soup, do not add the milk but cream the soup and ladle hot in sterilized hot jars and pressure cook at 10 lbs for 40 minutes later to make soup add same amount of milk as soup.

This is one of our favorites. Mary Grier my good friend said she hated goat's milk as she was enjoying this soup (with goat's milk) .You may add milk of your choice.

Cream of Potato Soup

3 Tbsp. grapeseed oil
2 medium diced onions
2 cups water
5 medium diced potatoes
1 Tbsp. dried parsley
1½ tsp. dried dill
Sea salt to taste
1 cup favorite milk

In the oil, cook the onion until soft. Add the water and the potatoes. Cook until potatoes are soft. Blend in blender. Return to pot. Add the parsley, dill, salt and milk.

You may do half in blender and add to the potatoes in the pot.

In place of potatoes, use 3 cups celery and 2 cups potatoes for Cream of Celery.

Cream of Carrot Soup

5 cups sliced carrots
4 Tbsp. Better Butter
1/3 cup purified water
¼ tsp. Chicolin®/stevia mix
1½ Tbsp. organic light spelt flour **or** potato flour
4 cups milk (a mix of goat's and rice milk)
4 Tbsp. organic lemon juice

Place carrots, onion, 2 Tbsp. butter in pot. Cook 5 minutes. Add water, sea salt and Chicolin mix. Cook 25 minutes or until soft. Blend ½ of carrots well and return to pot or blend all depending on how chunky you prefer. Combine spelt with milk. Combine this sauce to carrots and heat gently. Add lemon juice. Salt to taste.

Cream of Broccoli Soup

4 Tbsp. Better Butter
1 small chopped onion
1 crushed minced garlic clove
4 cups washed chopped broccoli stems diced very small
Sea salt to taste
3 cups vegetable broth
2 cups favorite milk
2 cups broccoli flowerets
½ tsp. dried basil

Melt butter in a large pot; add the onion and garlic. Cook until soft. Add the broccoli, salt and broth. Cook 15 minutes or until tender. Blend and return to pot and add the milk, flowerets and seasoning. Heat gently with the flowerets until cooked.

 Can be canned by just before adding the milk, place in

Cream of Fennel Soup

*GOOD FOR ALLERGIES, CANDIDA, CELIACS AND PEOPLE WITH DIABETES

1 Tbsp. grapeseed oil
1 cup of chopped fennel
3 shallots, diced
¼ cup red onion, chopped
Pinch of nutmeg and cayenne
6 cups of chicken broth
2 Tbsp. organic lemon juice
2 medium potatoes (diced)
1 cup favorite milk

In a large pot add oil, fennel, shallots & onions. Cook 5 to 10 minutes until soft. Add seasonings, careful with cayenne. You may omit it .Add broth, lemon juice and potatoes. Cook until tender, blend it until smooth in a blender and return to heat in pot.

Add the milk and warm it through.

Ah, C'est Delicieux!

Cream of Mushroom Soup

(This recipe is not for those who have Candida)

2 Tbsp. Better Butter
1 pound of mushrooms (washed)
1/3 cup organic light spelt **or** potato flour
½ tsp. sea salt
3 cups vegetable **or** chicken broth
3 cups favorite milk (rice, seed, soy or goat)

Cook mushrooms slowly in butter. Cover, reduce heat and simmer 20 minutes. Remove the mushrooms from the pan and set aside. Add flour to pan and make a roux, stirring to blend really well. Add salt, then broth and make a sauce. It should be fairly thick. Return mushrooms to the saucepan. At this point you may want to can it. If not, then add the milk slowly until you get the right thickness, simmer 5minutes. Adjust salt.

If canning this soup, double and triple the batch. Place in hot sterilized pint jars and place them in a pressure cooker for 40 minutes at 10 lbs. This will replace canned mushroom soup and can be used for entrees as well as a quick soup by adding an equal amount of your favorite milk (goat or rice or soy or seed or nut).

Cream of Celery Soup

2 Tbsp. grapeseed oil
1 medium diced onion
1¾ cup diced celery
3 Tbsp. light organic spelt **or** potato flour
3 cups vegetable **or** chicken broth
2 medium diced potatoes
¼ cup fresh parsley
½ tsp. sea salt
¼ tsp. celery seed
¼ tsp. paprika
1 cup favorite milk (soy, rice, seed, nut or goat)

In saucepan, add oil and cook onion and celery until soft. Add flour, broth, potatoes, parsley, salt, celery seed and paprika. Simmer 15 minutes until tender. In blender you may liquefy it all or a portion. Return to pot and add milk and heat. Serve warm.

If you want to can it, cook it down and do not add the milk. In hot sterilized pint jars pour the hot condensed soup in and seal. In pressure cooker, cook 40 minutes at 10 lbs. To use in casseroles add ¼ cup favorite milk. To use as soup, add even amount of milk.

Your own Cream of Chicken soup. Enjoy! Make a double or triple batch.

Cream of Chicken Soup

2 Tbsp. Better Butter
1 onion, diced
1 cup celery, diced
2 carrots, diced
4 cups purified water
2 organic chicken breasts cut in cubes (for vegetarian use chicken like broth instead of water)
1 tsp. seasoning salt
1 cup potatoes, shredded
2 cups favorite milk

In a large saucepan, add butter, onions, celery and carrots. Cook until soft. Add water and cubed chicken breasts. Bring to a boil and simmer 1 hour to make a rich broth. Add the seasoning salt and potatoes. Cook another 10 minutes. Place half in blender and blend until smooth. Blend the next half and return to pot. At this point, either add the milk or can the condensed soup in sterilized jars in pressure cooker for 40 minutes at 10 lbs.

If you canned this soup and you are ready to use for casseroles and entrees, add ½ cup milk of choice. To use as soup, add same amount of milk.

Creamed Sauces Solutions Collection

This collection contains dairy free sauces for times when you want to perk up your vegetables or desserts. We miss some of these foods when we are restricted, so it's nice to have a sauce to enhance our meals such as Béchamel, rich béchamel, moray, voloute, creamy Alfred-o, creamed kale and onion, creamed kohlrabi.

Perfect dessert sauces would include sweet cream sauce, orange cream sauce, creamy carob or chocolate sauce. These recipes will complement your meals.

Cream sauces are wonderful for dressing up vegetables or entrees as they add flavor and color to dishes that are otherwise dry.

They are used on pastas, rice, vegetables and casseroles. They can simply change simple foods into nouvelle cuisine.

We, who have difficulties with dairy or are vegan, are restricted from having most cream sauces. If you prepare them as directed in these recipes, you should have no trouble having a creamed dish now and then.

The sweet sauces are used for dressing up plain puddings and cakes. They add an interesting touch to a plain dessert especially if you use a bit of fruit.

I pray that you will enjoy these recipes and that they help you attain meals that will be more satisfying and that you will grow better and stronger each day feeling satisfied. God Bless as you prepares these foods for you and yours.

Rich Hollandaise Sauce

1 cup favorite milk (rice, nut, seed, soy or goat's)
1 Tbsp. spelt flour **or** potato flour
3 free range egg yolks
5 Tbsp. fresh organic lemon juice
3 Tbsp. Better Butter
Dash of cayenne

Liquefy all ingredients in blender for 2 minutes. In a double boiler, cook the sauce stirring until thick. Keep warm but not too hot. It's fast and easy. Serve over poached eggs, asparagus, artichoke or Eggs Benny.

Béchamel Sauce

The French Béchamel Sauce can be used in many ways such as on vegetables. It is called the "Mother Sauce". It is the basic sauce for all other cream sauces. It should always be made in a heavy saucepan so it does not scorch.

2 Tbsp. Better Butter
2 Tbsp. spelt flour **or** potato flour
1 cup favorite milk (soy, rice, nut or goat)
Sea salt to taste
Pinch nutmeg

Melt butter and flour. Make a roux. Watch closely. DO NOT BROWN. Add milk. Stir and season. Makes 1 cup.

Richer Béchamel Sauce

To the finished sauce previous, add 2 Tbsp. more of butter.

Mornay Sauce

To the finished Béchamel sauce, add ½ cup grated cheese. Stir over heat until cheese melts. Season with a little mustard.

Veloute´ Sauce

To prepare a non-dairy version of the Béchamel sauce, substitute the milk ingredient with one of the following; hot chicken, fish, vegetable or beef broth.

Cream Béchamel Sauce

To Béchamel sauce, add 3 Tbsp. heavy cream (¼ cup water +¼ cup nut or seed liquefied in blender).
1 onion ring

Leave onion in cream. Heat and remove onion.

Mustard Sauce

When making Béchamel sauce, add 1 tsp. dry mustard to flour when making roux. Continue as in Béchamel Sauce.

 Mustard sauce is excellent for fish and broiled meats.

Curry Sauce

When making Béchamel sauce, add 1 tsp. curry sauce to flour when making roux. Continue as in Béchamel Sauce.

Herb Sauce

To hot Béchamel sauce, add 1 tsp. fresh chopped minced herbs or ½ tsp. dry herbs. Let it sit 10 minutes to distribute flavor.

Alfredo Sauce

In a blender:

1¾ cups milk of choice
2 Tbsp. light organic spelt flour **or** potato flour
1 Tbsp. chicken seasoning **or** vegetarian chicken seasoning
½ tsp. each sea salt, onion powder
¼ tsp. dried basil

Blend until creamy. Bring to a slow boil. Remove. Add
¼ tsp. dried basil or 1 tsp. fresh basil.

 This is very good over pasta. Broccoli or mushrooms could be added. For creamier sauce, add ½ cup soy mozzarella cheese.

Creamed Kale & Onion Sauce

1½ lbs. roughly chopped kale
12 small white onions
¼ cup Better Butter
3 Tbsp. light organic spelt flour **or** potato flour
1½ cups favorite milk (nut, rice, soy seed or goat)
Sea salt

Cook washed kale until tender. Drain. Cook onions in water 15 minutes. In a medium saucepan, melt butter and flour, making a roux. Add milk Stir until creamy adding salt and pepper. Combine vegetables. Pour sauce over them.

Here's a tip: Cut the spine of the Kale Leaf
off with your knife after folding over,
and discard the tough stem.

Basic Cream Sauce

1 1/3 cups favorite milk (soy, rice, goat, nut or seed)
1 tsp. sea salt
1 Tbsp. chicken seasoning * 2 Tbsp. spelt flour **or** potato flour
¼ tsp. celery salt
½ tsp. onion powder
¼ tsp. garlic powder

Blend all ingredients in the blender. In a medium saucepan, bring to a boil. Stir until thick.

Creamed Kohlrabi Sauce

1½ pounds of Kohlrabi peeled and cubed
3 Tbsp. Better Butter
1 cup chicken broth
4 Tbsp. spelt flour **or** potato flour
1 cup cream (homemade cashew cream) blend 2x nuts to water
¼ cup fresh chopped parsley

Melt butter in large saucepan. Add kohlrabi. Cook 2 minutes. Add broth and simmer, covered, 10 minutes or until tender. Mix flour and milk until smooth. Add slowly stirring into the saucepan. Add parsley.

Sweet Cream Sauce

1 cup boiling favorite milk
1 tsp. Better Butter
2 free range egg whites, beaten
Pinch Chicolin®/stevia mix
1 tsp. cornstarch
½ cup cold favorite milk

In a medium saucepan, add butter to boiling milk. To beaten egg whites add chicolin mix and cornstarch. Gently fold egg white mixture to the boiling mix in saucepan. Add milk and cook until thick. This is one of the best cream sauces, try it! You'll really love it.

Orange Cream Sauce

1 cup orange juice
Juice of ½ lemon
1½ Tbsp. Chicolin®/stevia mix
¼ tsp. orange rind
½ tsp. sea salt
2 Tbsp. corn or tapioca starch
½ cup whipped tofu cream *see below for recipe

Heat juices & chicolin mix to a boil. Mix starch with a little cold water to make a paste. Add to juice stirring until clear. Remove from heat. Chill; add to whipped tofu. (1 package tofu, 3 Tbsp. chicolin mix, 2 tsp. lemon juice in blender. Slowly add ½ cup grapeseed oil.) 💡 Perfect for cakes, puddings and fruit.

Creamy Hot Chocolate or Carob Sauce

3 unsweetened chocolate squares **or** 1cup carob chips
2 cups favorite milk (soy, rice or goat)
3 Tbsp. Chicolin®/stevia mix
¼ cup light organic spelt flour **or** tapioca starch
¼ tsp. sea salt
1 tsp. vanilla extract
1Tbsp. Better Butter

Melt chocolate or carob chips over hot water. Combine milk, chicolin mix, flour (or starch) and salt. Add enough of the hot chocolate to make a smooth paste. Add remaining chocolate cooking 10 minutes until thick and smooth. Remove from heat. Add butter. Serve over homemade ice cream or Rice Dream Ice Cream. Sometimes this will thicken; just adds a little more milk.

💡 Can also be used in Rice Dream milk to make hot chocolate or chocolate milk.

Casual Condiments Collection

These are fun to make and we are enjoying them. They are ideal for the allergic or Candida and Diabetic sufferers. There is no sugar or vinegar in these recipes. These are usually the "forbidden foods" for Candida sufferers.

Miss Ketchup? How about pickles? One of the big struggles with Candida is having to give up condiments. For some with allergies to sugar and vinegar you also have to be cut it from your diet.

With these recipes you can now enjoy some of the forbidden foods. You can dress up some of your favorite sandwiches. The great thing about these recipes is that everyone can enjoy them whether they have health issues or not.

 Salad dressings should be made with Olive oil and fresh organic lemon juice base and Chicolin®/stevia used as a sweetener. Avoid vinegar. Also to replace any fruit vinegar, add pure fruit juice to lemon juice.

Ezee Mayo

1¼ cup purified water
1/3cup light organic spelt flour
½ tsp. sea salt
¼ tsp. onion powder
½ tsp. Chicolin®/stevia mix
½ crushed minced clove garlic* opt.
½ cup grapeseed oil
2 Tbsp. organic lemon juice

In a saucepan, place all but the oil and lemon juice. Cook until thick. Cool. In a blender, slowly add the oil. When done, stir in lemon juice. Chill. Makes 1½ cup. Keeps about 1 week.

EZ Tomato Catsup

2 cups tomato juice
1 can tomato sauce **or** 4 cups tomato juice
¾ cup lemon juice
3Tbsp. Chicolin®/stevia mix
1 tsp. sea salt
Pinch tsp. cinnamon
1 small can tomato paste

Combine the tomato sauce, juice, in a large saucepan and bring it to a boil. Watch closely. Simmer about 1 ¼ hour .Add the lemon juice and seasonings. Cook a few more hours on simmer until reduced to half.

Cranberry Sauce

4 cups washed cranberries
½ cup purified water
6 Tbsp. Chicolin®/stevia mix

Place the water with the Chicolin in a saucepan and bring to a boil. Cook 5 minutes, on simmer. Add washed and picked over cranberries. Cook until berries are soft.

Agave Mustard

1 Tbsp. light organic spelt flour **or** potato flour
¼ cup fresh organic lemon juice
¼ cup purified water
1 Tbsp. Agave nectar (organic sweetener/sugar substitute)
½ tsp. sea salt
1 Tbsp. dry mustard
¼ tsp. turmeric

Mix all ingredients & bring to boil, lower heat & stir until thick. You may double or triple the batch. While still hot, place in hot sterilized jars and process in hot water 10 minutes.

Homemade Chili Sauce

3 large chopped organic tomatoes
2 medium green apples peeled and grated
1 medium onion diced fine
¼ cup organic lemon juice
1½ Tbsp. Chicolin®/stevia mix
½ tsp. cinnamon
½ tsp. sea salt

In a large saucepan add all the ingredients and bring to a boil. Simmer for 2 ½ hours on low. Remove and pour into a sterilized jar. Seal. This can be doubled and also done in the crock-pot.

Homemade Lemon Mustard

1 Tbsp. turmeric
2 Tbsp. grapeseed oil
1 tsp. sea salt
1 cup purified water
12 Tbsp. organic light spelt flour

Blend all of the above ingredients well and cook over medium heat until thick. Cool. Meanwhile in blender, add 2 fresh cloves of garlic add the above mustard and whirl and blend until garlic is well mixed. Slowly add 2/3 cup of fresh organic lemon juice.
Place in sterilized jars and seal by hot water bath for 10 minutes.

Tartar Sauce

½ cup homemade mayonnaise
2 Tbsp. minced dill pickles
2 tsp. minced red pimento
1 tsp. each chopped onion, parsley **and** organic lemon juice

Mix all well. Place in a small jar. Makes 4 oz.

BBQ Sauce

1 cup chopped onion
1 cup homemade ketchup*
2/3 cup purified water +½ cup organic lemon juice
½ cup Chicolin®/stevia mix
1 tsp. chili powder
1 tsp. sea salt

In a saucepan place all ingredients and bring to a boil. Simmer 10 minutes.

Sweet Sour Sauce

3 cups unsweetened pineapple juice
2/3 cup homemade ketchup
1 can drained pineapple chunks + 1 diced green pepper
3 Tbsp. Bragg's™ all purpose seasoning
1 tsp. Chicolin®/stevia mix
2 Tbsp. fresh lemon juice
2 Tbsp. corn, tapioca **or** arrowroot starch
½ cup purified water

In a small saucepan combine pineapple juice, ketchup, pineapples, pepper, Bragg's, chicolin and lemon juice. Bring to a boil. Mix the starch into water until smooth. Add slowly stirring. Cook until smooth and thick. Serve hot.

The Home of 2P's Health Kitchen

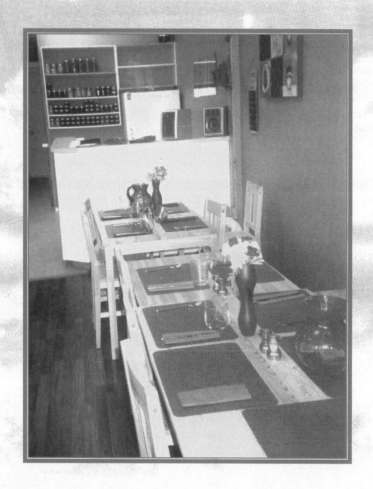

Vernon, British Columbia Canada

The Bread Bin Collection

This Collection will give you a variety of bread replacements so that you can enjoy toast and sandwiches without yeast or wheat. Spelt is a form of wheat but can be used by many. Please get checked to see if you are able to use it. Nothing beats the wonderful smell of homemade bread. In this collection you will find a variety of recipes all yeast free. The versatility of the mixes enables you to prepare other delicious recipes When we are limited it's good to have a variety such as a corn mix for muffins, corn bread and waffles. In this collection you will find breads to munch on with soup or scones for early morning to be enjoyed with a homemade jam or jelly. Tortillas are one of my favorites as they can be used as a wrap if you make them at least 6" in diameter and after making them you can keep them warm in the oven then they fold nicely. Have fun experimenting with them until you get them to your liking. The recipe is a base and in time you will enjoy them many ways. Soda bread is a nice change and the biscuit recipe resembles Bisquick™. So any recipe that asks for Bisquick, this may be used in its place. This is a collection of recipes for those who have allergies or Candida. There is no sugar, no dairy, no yeast and no wheat in the breads. Someone asked, "What do you have in the bread?"

2 Hour Buns

Note: This is the only exception of bread with yeast in this collection of recipes.

3 cups warm purified water
2 free range eggs, beaten
1/3 cup Better Butter, melted
1 large Tbsp. Chicolin®/stevia mix
1 Tbsp. sea salt
3 Tbsp. instant yeast
7 - 8 cups spelt flour (a little at a time)

Preheat oven to 375°. In a small bowl add the warm water, beaten eggs and melted butter. Beat and set aside. In a large bowl, mix all remaining ingredients. Make a well and pour the water mixture in. Mix well. Knead and make into a ball. Grease a bowl, add dough, let rise 15 minutes and knead. Do this 4 times in all at 15-minute intervals. Make into buns. Make them the size you want. Set on a greased cookie sheet and let rise 30 minutes. Bake about 25 minutes until golden. Makes good bread. All you need to do is shape it into 2 loaves and place in loaf pans and bake same as the buns.

Cinnamon Buns

Use the same recipe as "2 Hour Buns". Roll out the dough. You may make half buns or 1 bread loaf and a batch of buns. After rolling half the dough, butter it with Earth Balance Butter or Better Butter and sprinkle 3Tbps.Chicolin/Stevia-sprinkle cinnamon on it. Roll and cut. Optional: You may ice with Butter Frosting recipe found in the "Cool Cakes" section (look up in index at that back of the book for the recipe).

Pineapple Bread

Use the same recipe as "2 Hour Buns". Roll ¼ of the dough. Butter it then add pineapple chunks. Cook & thicken juice with 2 Tbsp. Spelt or starch and 1 Tbsp. Chicolin®/stevia. Cover pineapple with dough cut vent holes then bake 25 minutes. Drizzle with sauce.

Baking Powder Biscuit

2 cups spelt organic flour
4 tsp. homemade Baking Powder
½ tsp. sea salt
1/3 cup coconut oil or Earth Balance Butter or Better Butter
2/3 cup milk of choice

Preheat oven 450°. Mix flour, baking powder and salt. Cut in the shortening or butter and mix until it resembles oatmeal. Add milk. Mix and gently pat it down. It will be soft so add a little more flour. Using a small glass cut them into rounds and place on an **ungreased** cookie sheet and bake between 10 – 15 minutes. You can make a variety of biscuits by adding seeds or herbs of choice.

Raisin Scones

1 cup organic spelt flour +½ cup corn flour *opt.
¼ tsp Chicolin®/stevia mix
½ tsp. sea salt
4 Tbsp. Better Butter or 3 Tbsp. coconut oil
½ cup organic raisins * for those who can
2 free range eggs well-beaten **or** 6 Tbsp. Flax Gel
½ cup milk of choice (goat, grain, nut, rice, seed or soy)

Preheat oven to 450°. Mix as listed above. Make into 2 balls, flatten, and cut into wedges. Bake 15 minutes.

Yeast Free Loaf Mix

9 cups of light organic spelt flour **or**
2 cups corn flour **and** 7 cups spelt **or**
3 cups spelt **and** 6 cups whole wheat (your choice)
5 Tbsp. homemade Baking Powder
4 Tbsp. soda
¾ Tbsp. sea salt

Mix all the ingredients together and store in cool place or freezer. (Choose the flour mix you prefer)

Yeast Free Loaf

2 free range eggs or 6 Tbsp. Flax Gel
2 cups preferred milk
½ tsp. Chicolin®/stevia mix
4 cups yeast free loaf mix (see above recipe)

Preheat oven to 350°. Beat eggs and add remaining ingredients. Pour into an oiled bread pan and bake 45 minutes or until brown and done. Remove from pan and lay on its side to cool.

 These breads are not exactly like your yeast breads. They are more like cake bread.

Yeast Free Pumpkin Loaf

1½ cups pumpkin puree
1 tsp. Chicolin®/stevia mix
½ tsp. pumpkin pie spice
½ cup dried instant potato flakes
2½ cups Yeast-Free Loaf mix

Preheat oven to 350°. Combine all ingredients and spoon in a greased bread pan. Bake for 1 hour.

Basic Cornmeal Mix

6 cups cornmeal
3 cups light organic spelt flour
1cup rice bran
3½ Tbsp. homemade Baking Powder
2 tsp. sea salt

Combine all ingredients together. Mix well. Keep in a sealed container in a cool place or freezer.

"It takes adjustment but we do not have a choice so we adapt to a different way of eating. If I would be free of my allergies tomorrow I would still maintain the way I eat now."
Jeannine '2p' Edwards

Easy Corn Bread

1 free range egg or 3 Tbsp. Flax Gel
4 Tbsp. or coconut oil or grapeseed oil
1 cup soy, rice, nut or goat's milk (or a mixture)
1¾ cups Basic Cornmeal mix (see previous recipe)

Preheat oven to 425°. Beat egg and combine the remaining ingredients. Bake for 35 minutes.

Easier Corn Muffins

1 free range egg or 3 Tbsp. Flax Gel
4 Tbsp. grapeseed oil
½ tsp. Chicolin®/stevia mix
1 cup soy, rice, nut **or** goat's milk (or a mixture)
1¾ cups Basic Cornmeal mix

Preheat oven 425°. Beat egg and add remaining ingredients. Mix and spoon into greased muffin tins. Bake 30 minutes.

Corn Waffles

1 free range egg or 3 Tbsp. Flax gel
 4 Tbsp. coconut oil or Better Butter
1 cup soy, rice, nut **or** goat's milk (or a mixture)
2½ cups Basic Cornmeal mix
½ tsp. soda

Preheat waffle iron. Beat egg and add remaining ingredients. Pour on hot waffle iron. Cook until brown. Especially crispy on the outside and tender in the middle!

Garlic and Onion Bread

3½ cups light organic spelt flour
1 tsp. Chicolin®/stevia mix
1 Tbsp. homemade Baking Powder
1½ tsp. sea salt
¼ cup dried onion flakes
¼ cup coconut oil **or** Better Butter
1¼ cup soy, rice, nut **or** goat's milk (or a mixture)
1 range free egg or 3 Tbsp. Flax Gel
2 small cloves crushed garlic

About 2 hours before serving preheat oven to 375° Grease a 9x5-loaf pan. In a large bowl, with fork, mix flour, chicolin mix, baking powder, salt and onion flakes. Cut in butter and mix until coarse. Set aside. In a small bowl, mix milk, egg and garlic. Add to flour mix. The dough will be stiff and sticky. Knead then shape into loaf and slash top 6 times 1/4 inch deep. Bake on sheet 1 hour and 10 minutes. Cool 1/2 hour.

Spelt Scones

2 cups light organic spelt **or** other flour **or** part corn
½ tsp. sea salt
4 tsp. homemade Baking Powder
6 Tbsp. coconut oil **or** cold Better Butter
¾ cup cold rice **or** goat's milk

Both butter and milk should be very cold. This will make the scones flakier.

Preheat oven to 450°. Mix dry ingredients together. Cut in butter with pastry cutter until the size of peas. Add milk and mix lightly with fork. Be very gentle and do not overwork. Pat and form into a circle. Cut into wedges and place on increased cookie sheet. Bake 17 minutes.

Can be flavored with 1 tsp. herbs or 1 tsp. orange peel and 1 cup of cranberries after cutting the butter.

Treasured Tortillas

2 cups light organic spelt flour **or** other flour mixture
½ tsp. sea salt
3 Tbsp. coconut oil **or** grapeseed oil
½ cup purified water

Mix all ingredients together. Roll out cut into circles. Pan fry in very little Grape seed oil. Fry both sides Keep warm to roll. Enjoy this treasured tortilla recipe rolled up with any filling your heart desires.

Spelt Soda Bread

4 cups light organic spelt flour
1 tsp. Chicolin®/stevia mix
2 tsp. homemade Baking Powder
1 tsp. soda
1 free range egg **or** 3 Tbsp. Flax Gel
2 cups soy, rice, nut **or** goat's milk plus 2 tsp. lemon juice
¼ cup spelt flakes

Preheat oven to 375°. Mix first 4 ingredients together. In a separate bowl, mix milk and egg together. Combine wet and dry. Mix. Dust board with spelt flakes. Knead dough. Let rest; place on greased cookie sheet. Make an X on top. Bake 45-50 minutes. Serve warm.

Easy Biscuit Mix

1cup each coconut oil **and** Better Butter
9 cups light organic spelt flour **or** 7 cups spelt & 2 cups corn flour
1 Tbsp. sea salt
¼ cup homemade Baking Powder

Mix well. Keep in an airtight container. Store in refrigerator or freezer.

 There are many other recipes you can make from this mix.

Baking Powder Biscuits

2 1/3 cup Biscuit mix
2 tsp. homemade Baking Powder
¼ cup coconut **or** vegetable shortening
2/3 cup soy, rice, nut **or** goat's milk

Preheat oven to 425°. Mix all ingredients until soft dough is formed. Gently smooth into a ball. Pat ½ inch thick. Cut with 3" circle cutter. Bake until golden brown on an **ungreased** cookie sheet for 10 minutes.

Pancakes & Crepes Collection

Have you ever had guests for breakfast and felt the best thing to offer was a stack of fluffy pancakes, dab of butter and a fruit sauce? Have you ever enjoyed a small delicate light crepe filled with fruit and a whipped topping on a weekend morning? Some unsweetened crepes are very tasty filled with creamed fillings for a light luncheon. Who can resist golden waffles on a platter surrounded with glistening fruit? Because of allergies to milk, wheat and sugar, they seem very remote and unattainable but we, too, can enjoy them. Here's how - by replacing the items we can't have with some that are better for us. Will you join me and enjoy some of these recipes? Come, my friends as you travel on the road of recovery and well being.

God bless and keep you well ~ Jeannine '2P' Edwards

Fluffy Pancakes

1¼ cups light organic spelt flour
1 tsp. homemade Baking Powder
1 Tbsp. soda
½ tsp. sea salt
3 beaten free range egg yolks
1½ cups sour milk (the milk + 2 tsp. lemon juice)
3 Tbsp. melted Better Butter
3 egg whites beaten until stiff

Sift all dry ingredients and set aside. Make a well in center of mix add the egg yolks, milk and butter. Whip until light and fluffy. If too stiff add more milk. Must be thick. Fold in the egg whites. Bake on hot griddle. Cook until bubbles then turn over.

Baked Pancakes

2 free range eggs **or** 6 Tbsp. Flax Gel
½ cup favorite milk (rice, soy, goat, seed or nut)
½ cup light organic spelt flour
¼ tsp. nutmeg
4 Tbsp. Better Butter
1 Tbsp. Chicolin®/stevia mix
Juice of ½ fresh organic lemon

Preheat oven 425°. Mix eggs and milk; add flour and nutmeg. Leave the batter lumpy. Melt butter in a 12" skillet. Pour in batter. Bake 12 to 20 minutes until golden brown. Remove from oven and sprinkle chicolin mix, return to oven a few minutes. Remove again and sprinkle lemon juice. Cut in wedges and serve with homemade jam.

Biscuit Mix Crepes

¾ cup Biscuit mix (see previous recipe)
2 eggs **or** 6 Tbsp. flax gel
¾ cup soy, rice, nut **or** goat's milk

Beat all ingredients together until smooth. For each crepe, pour 2 Tbsp. of mixture in a hot skillet turning pan until it is evenly spread out. Cook one side until the edge slightly curls. Turn cooking other side until golden brown. Keep warm.

Cherry Sauce

¾ cup cherry juice (from canned cherries)
1/8 tsp. sea salt
1½ Tbsp. Chicolin®/stevia
1½ tsp. corn or arrowroot or tapioca starch
¼ jar canned homemade cherries
2 Tbsp. Better Butter
1 Tbsp. Fresh organic lemon juice

Heat the juice, salt, chicolin mix and starch until it thickens. Add cherries, lemon juice and butter Heat through and serve warm. This is good on any dessert or breakfast pancake as an extra added sauce!

Pumpkin Puff Pancakes

1 cup favorite milk
2 free range egg yolks
½ cup pumpkin
2 Tbsp. grapeseed oil
1cup light organic spelt flour
½ tsp. Chicolin®/stevia mix
2 tsp. homemade Baking Powder
½ tsp. sea salt
1 tsp. cinnamon
2 egg whites stiffly beaten

In a bowl, beat egg yolks, pumpkin, oil and milk. Add the dry ingredients. Fold in egg whites. Cook on grill by ¼ cup measure. Serve hot with Better Butter and hot applesauce.

Hot Apple Sauce

¾ cup apple juice
3 Tbsp. Chicolin®/stevia mix
2 Tbsp. Better Butter **or** Earth Balance Butter
½ tsp. fresh organic lemon juice
1/8 tsp. cinnamon
1/8 tsp. nutmeg

Bring all to a boil and simmer to reduce to 1 cup. Let sit 30 minutes or make the evening before. Heat and serve.

Buckwheat/Spelt Pancake Mix

2½ cups organic spelt flour
5½ cups buckwheat flour
1 tsp. sea salt
6 Tbsp. homemade Baking Powder

Mix and keep cool in refrigerator or freezer. Very good.

Buckwheat Pancakes

1 free range egg or 3 Tbsp. Flax Gel
1 cup milk (goat, soy, rice, nut or seed)
1 cup buckwheat/spelt pancake mix
(If using 3 Tbsp. Flax Gel, * add ¼ tsp. more of homemade Baking Powder)

Mix and cook on griddle or pan. Serve with syrup, fruit or sauce.

Apple Buckwheat Pancakes

3 eggs **or** 9 Tbsp. Flax Gel
1cup pure unsweetened apple juice
1 cup buckwheat/spelt pancake mix

Mix and cook. Serve with applesauce.

Buckwheat and Blueberry Pancakes

1 cup favorite milk
1 free range egg **or** 3 Tbsp. Flax Gel
½ cup buckwheat/spelt pancake mix
2/3 cup blueberries

Mix milk, egg and buckwheat mix. Add berries. Cook on grill. Serve with blueberry sauce.

Corn Meal Waffles

2 free range egg yolks
2 cups favorite sour milk
1cup light organic spelt flour
¾ cups corn meal
2 tsp. homemade Baking Powder
1 tsp. soda
1½ tsp. sea salt
½ tsp. Chicolin®/stevia mix
¼ cup ground flaxseed
6 Tbsp. melted Better Butter
2 beaten egg whites

Beat yolks with milk. Combine all dry ingredients and add to egg mixture. Blend until smooth. Add melted butter. Fold in egg whites. Cook in hot waffle iron. Makes 1 dozen.

Waffles

1¾ cups favorite milk
3 free range egg yolks
2 cups organic spelt flour
4 tsp. homemade Baking Powder
¼ tsp. sea salt
½ cup melted Better Butter
3 beaten egg whites

Add milk to well beaten eggs yolks. Stir in the dry ingredients. Add melted butter and fold in egg whites. Pour into waffle iron and cook until golden.

Blueberry or Strawberry Sauce

2 cups strawberries or blueberries
2 Tbsp. Chicolin®/stevia mix
2 Tbsp. corn **or** tapioca **or** arrowroot starch

Cook together until thick and clear. Serve with pancakes or waffles. Other fruit can be substituted.

Raspberry Sauce

2 cups raspberries
2 Tbsp. Chicolin®/stevia mix
2 Tbsp. arrowroot, tapioca **or** cornstarch
½ cup purified water
1 tsp. fresh organic *lemon* juice

Combine all ingredients and cook until thick. Serve warm.

Swedish Crepes

1½ cups light organic spelt flour
2 cups rice milk (vanilla for sweet or original for plain)
3 free range farm eggs
2 Tbsp. Earth Balance Butter **or** other (melted)

Beat eggs. Add the milk and flour alternatively. Add butter. Using a non-stick pan pour some batter (it should be thin and tip the pan to cover the bottom. Cook one side and turn over for a few seconds. Good stuffed with fruit and a sweet cream sauce or for luncheon with favorite meat or veggie cream filling.

Mighty Muffins Collection

These muffins are made with an array of vegetables and fruit. You will find a mixture of muffins to please every taste. You will notice the muffins are not made to be extremely sweet as we have our Candida friends in mind, as well as Allergic and Diabetic sufferers.

Maybe you are not having health problems but would like to protect yourself as you have read and heard about foods that are good and those who are not beneficial.

Whatever the case, I invite you to try these recipes. My prayer is that you will enjoy them and find them appealing and satisfying.

Have you missed having a muffin because you could not have wheat flour or sugar? Well here are some recipes to add to your collection and you will be able to have them if you are Diabetic, Allergic or suffer from Candida. They are sugarless and dairy free and are made with spelt flour.

Mighty muffins to the rescue. Small but powerfully good. We have all kinds - Bran, Blueberry, Cranberry Combo, Carrot, Flaxseed/ Carrot, Pineapple, and Pumpkin/Sunflower. Voila!

They can be made with other flours as well, such as Amaranth, Quinoa, Corn or Kamut. They are nice in the morning or with tea in the afternoon or for a snack. Enjoy!

Pans should be oiled or lined with paper cup liners.

Apple and Cranberry Muffins

½ cup of Better Butter **or** 1/3 cup coconut oil
2 free range eggs **or** 6 Tbsp. Flax Gel
¼ cup pure organic apple juice
1 cup spelt flakes ground in blender (not fine but course)
1½ cups light organic spelt flour
½ tsp. each salt, soda and cinnamon
4 Tbsp. Chicolin®/stevia mix
4 tsp. homemade Baking Powder
1 cup each apple sauce and dried cranberries
½ cup raw organic sunflower seeds

Preheat oven 350°. Mix butter or oil with the eggs or gel. Mix all the dry ingredients together adding the cranberries and seeds. Mix into the egg mixture adding the apples last. Place in lined muffin cups and bake 35 minutes.

Make your own applesauce by cooking 2 apples in a little apple juice until cooked then mash.

These muffins are better on the second day. Try changing the apple juice for pure cherry juice and replacing the cranberries with dried cherries.

Zucchini Muffins

¼ cup grapeseed oil or coconut oil
2/3 cups purified water
1 beaten egg or 3 Tbsp. Flax Gel
½ cup soymilk (powder)
2½ cups light organic spelt flour **or** 2 cups spelt+½ cup corn
1 tsp. sea salt
2 tsp. homemade Baking Powder
¾ Tbsp. Chicolin®/stevia mix
1 cup shredded zucchini

Preheat oven to 400°. In a lg. bowl, combine oil, water, egg, milk powder and zucchini. Add the flour, salt, baking powder and chicolin mix. Do not beat. Mix gently, adding the zucchini. Bake 20 to 25 minutes. 🔔 If you have an allergy to soy you may omit the water and powder and use 1cup favorite milk.

Rice Bran Muffins

1½ cups rice bran
1½ cups vanilla rice milk
1½ Tbsp. Chicolin®/stevia mix
3 Tbsp. Flax Gel **or** 1 organic free range egg
½ cup raisins **or** diced dates
1/3cup blackstrap molasses
1¼ cups spelt flour
2 tsp. homemade Baking Powder
¼ tsp. sea salt

Preheat oven to 375°. Combine 1½ cups each rice bran and milk and set aside for 10 minutes. Add all other ingredients together. Mix gently. Spoon in muffin tins and bake 25 minutes. Cool.

Pineapple Muffins

1 cup unsweetened pineapple juice
1 beaten free range egg **or** 3 Tbsp. Flax Gel
¼ cups shortening **or** coconut oil
2 cups light organic spelt flour
1 Tbsp. Chicolin®/stevia mix
4 tsp. homemade Baking Powder
½ tsp. sea salt
½ tsp. Chicolin®/stevia mix +1 tsp. lemon grated rind

Preheat oven to 400°. In a bowl, combine dry ingredients and set aside. In another bowl, mix oil, egg and pineapple juice. Add the dry ingredient Sprinkle mix of chicolin and rind on top muffins. Bake 20 to 25 minutes.

Blueberry Muffins

1¾ cups spelt **or** other flour (mix of spelt and corn)
2½ tsp. homemade Baking Powder
¾ Tbsp. Chicolin®/stevia mix
¾ tsp. sea salt
1 well beaten free range egg **or** 1 Tbsp. Flax Gel
1/3 cup grapeseed oil **or** coconut oil
¾ cup favorite milk
1cup blueberries (fresh or frozen)

Preheat oven to 400°. In a bowl, mix flour, baking powder, chicolin mix and salt. Set aside. In a large bowl, combine egg, oil, and milk. Add the flour mixture and mix gently adding the blueberries. Bake 25 minutes.

Flaxseed/ Carrot Muffin

2/3 cup flaxseed, milled in a coffee grinder
1cup favorite milk
1 tsp. lemon juice
1 Granny Smith apple, grated
4 Tbsp. grapeseed oil **or** coconut oil
1 free range egg **or** replacer
2 cups carrot, shredded
½ tsp. vanilla extract
2 cups light organic spelt **or** other flour
4 tsp. homemade Baking Powder
3 Tbsp. Chicolin®/stevia mix
¼ tsp. sea salt
1 tsp. cinnamon
¼ cup unsweetened coconut
¼ cup nuts **or** sunflower seeds
¼ cup raisins *optional

Preheat oven to 375°. In a large bowl, add milk and lemon juice to flaxseed. Leave 10 minutes. Add next 5 ingredients and set aside. In a separate bowl, sift dry ingredients including chicolin and add to wet mixture. Spoon into prepared muffin pans. Bake 30 minutes. This recipe is especially good for the eye sight and the liver. Yummy, of course too.

Flax Seeds are a great Liver Cleanser…

Flax Seeds ~ Keep them whole until you use them.
Store them in a closed jar in the cupboard to keep them fresh.

Cranberry Combo Muffins

1 cup mashed banana **or** applesauce
1 egg or 3 Tbsp. Flax Gel
¾ cup favorite milk
1½ Tbsp. Chicolin®/stevia mix
1/3 cup grapeseed oil **or** coconut oil
1½ cups 100% bran cereal **or** grapenuts cereal **or** rice bran
2 cups light organic spelt flour **or** other
½ cup nuts **or** seeds
1 Tbsp. homemade Baking Powder
½ tsp. sea salt
½ tsp. cinnamon
¾ cup cranberry sauce (set aside) homemade

Preheat oven to 400°. Mix banana or applesauce with the egg, milk, chicolin mix and oil. Add the bran and let sit 10 minutes. Mix the flour, nuts or seeds, baking powder, salt and cinnamon together. You can also add the chicolin in this instead of to the egg mixture, as it will mix better. Mix them all together and spoon to fill 1/2 muffin tin then add 1 Tbsp. cranberry sauce then cover with more batter. Bake 25 minutes.

Organic Cranberries in their
Natural state before they are picked.

Cranberries are especially good for the kidneys and urinary tract.

Jiffy Jams & Gelatins Collection

This Collection is a selection of various jams and jellies to please the jam lovers. This assortment varies from jam to gelatins. Try it with toast and muffins. Or, enjoy a cold bowl of homemade Jell-O (without the sugar!) on a hot summer day. You could also have a light pumpkin bar for a snack or dessert. At the price of sugarless jams, it is more economical to make your own. It is easy.

Most jams are easy to make. The problem is most are very sweet and require a lot of sugar. We cannot tolerate them with our health problems.

There are jams on the market that are "no sugar added" made from concentrated fruit juices. Unfortunately, the concentrated juices have sugar. Of course the sugar is not added per say, but it is in the sweetener (the juice). Chemical sweeteners are used in some jams. I, for one, stay clear from these sweeteners.

The recipes that follow will be of different ways of preparation.

I have found a (no sugar needed) pectin from the Bernadin Company that makes really easy and good jam. I am blessed with my own grapes so I made juice and used it for jelly.

Grape Jelly

4 cups grape juice (concord sweet or plain)
If plain add 4 Tbsp. Chicolin®/stevia
1 pkg. no sugar pectin

Place all ingredients into a medium saucepan and boil 5 minutes. Keep hot. Pour in 4 hot sterilized pint jars. Seal. Place in hot water bath (a pot with hot water). Boil 10 minutes.

Canning

Also I can my own fruit with Chicolin®/stevia mix by washing my fruit then sterilizing my pint jars. I then pack the fruit in and add 1tsp. Chicolin® mix to the jar and then fill with boiling water leaving an inch from the top. Cover and seal with new lids and place in kettle of boiling water.

Apples, strawberries, 10 minutes
Berries, cherries, pineapple and plums, 15 minutes
Apricots, peaches and pears, 25 minutes.

You can also make pies from these canned fruits. See * *Plentiful Pies Collection.*

Jiffy Jam

4 or 5 organic unsulfured pineapple rings
2 cups fresh or frozen fruit

Cut the rings into bite-sized pieces. Combine all. Let sit overnight. Place in blender and blend thoroughly.
Makes 2 ½ cups

There are many kinds of jams. This one is uncooked and you may choose any fruit that is available – fresh or frozen. It is recommended to keep refrigerated and to use up within 3 days because it does not contain preservatives.

Jams

Some will be prepared with gelatin, some with pectin, some with neither (when you have no pectin or gelatin in the house), some uncooked but blended and some with the amazing Monosa™ product making it very easy and very good.

Oh, the smell of bread toasting in the morning, and the thought of chunks of sweet strawberries, golden peaches and apricots, red raspberries, and delectable blueberries.

Jars should be washed then placed in boiling water on stove as well as covers and new lids. Check to ensure there is no cracks or nicks. Some just need sealing by covering jar tightly, others need a hot bath by placing filled sealed jars in hot water for a period of 10 minute.

~Bon Appetite~

Cherry Jam

½ cup unsweetened pineapple juice
2 pint of pitted sweet cherries
½ unpeeled organic lemon (quartered)
5 kernels from cherry pits (break pit and extract kernel)
6 Tbsp. Chicolin®/stevia mix

In a blender add juice, 1 pint of cherries, lemon and kernels. Cover blender and blend until it is all liquefied.
Pour into a broad flat saucepan. Bring to a boil. Stir in the other pint of cherries with the chicolin mix. Cook 40 minutes until a drop of jam is stiff on a cold plate. Pour into hot jars, seal and cool.
Yields 5 (6oz) jars.

Strawberry Jam

½ cup pure water
2 cups unsweetened fresh or canned pineapple (diced)
1 quart washed and hulled strawberries
9 Tbsp. Chicolin®/stevia mix

In a blender, liquefy water and pineapple. Pour into a large flat saucepan and bring it to a boil. Add strawberries and chicolin. Cook 40 minutes then check to see if a drip will stiffen when dropped on a cold plate. Pour into hot jars and seal. Cool.
Yields 4 (6oz) jars.

Pectin Jams

I am so happy to tell you that I found this product a few years ago. It makes such lovely jams and is so easy it is unreal. I love it!
It is called POMONA'S UNIVERSAL PECTIN. It jells with any amount of sugar or sweetener. It is not to say that the other recipes are not good but for those who don't want to fuss, this is it. It contains a large pkg. of pectin and a small pkg. of calcium that helps gel the pectin.

Take ½ tsp. calcium in package.
½ cup water and shake Store in fridge. Keeps several months. Shake well before using. Directions are enclosed.

Strawberry or Raspberry Jam

4 cups washed hulled mashed berries
4 Tbsp. Chicolin®/stevia mix
2 tsp. pectin powder
2 tsp. calcium water

Prepare 5-pint jars. Place prepared fruit in a saucepan with the calcium water. Bring to a boil. Mix pectin powder and chicolin mix together and add to the fruit Beat vigorously. Bring to a boil. Place in hot jars and seal Wipe jars. Remember always fill your jars and leave 1/2" from the top. Boil in hot bath 5 minutes (hot water in large pot).

Concord Grape Jelly

3½ pounds concord grapes
¼ cup fresh organic lemon juice
4 tsp. calcium water (from Ponomo)
2 Tbsp. Chicolin®/stevia mix
4 tsp. pectin powder

Mash grapes and simmer 10 minutes. Place in jelly bag or strainer to make 4 cups grape juice. Leave grape juice overnight in the fridge. In saucepan, add grape juice, lemon juice and calcium water. Stir in chicolin mix with the pectin mixing really well until dissolved. Bring to a boil 5 minutes and pour into 5 pint sterilized hot jars. Seal. Process in hot water for 5 minutes.

Pectin Jell-O

4 cups of favorite fruit juice
Sweeten to taste with Chicolin®/stevia mix **or** Agave Nectar (organic sweetener/sugar replacement)
4 tsp. calcium water (from Ponomo)
1 cup boiling water
4 tsp. pectin powder (from Ponomo)

Sweeten fruit juice to taste. Add calcium water. In the blender, add boiling water and pectin. Mix fruit juice with it. Blend until all dissolved. Add all together pour into a large bowl or individual small bowls. Let set in the fridge.

Gelatin Based Desserts

Almond Jell-O/Fruit

4 cups pure water
½ oz agar agar
1½ Tbsp. Chicolin®/stevia mix **or** agave nectar
1 tsp. almond extract
2 cups goat **or** rice **or** nut milk

Bring 4 cups pure water to a boil. Dissolve agar agar and chicolin mix. Boil 5 minutes. Turn heat off. Add extract and milk. Stir well. Pour in a square pan. Put in the top freezer of the fridge 30 minutes. Cut into 1" squares and serve with your favorite fruit.

Strawberry Mousse

1 envelope **or** 1Tbsp. unflavored gelatin
¼ cup orange **or** lemon juice
3 cups fresh washed hulled strawberries
¾ Tbsp. Chicolin®/stevia mix
4 egg whites

Combine gelatin with juice. Let stand 5 minutes in small pan. Warm until dissolved. In a blender, add strawberries with chicolin. Puree. Should be 1½ cups. Transfer in a bowl-adding gelatin. Whip egg whites until stiff. Mix in the gelatin and berry mix. Serve chilled.

Apple-Pumpkin Bars

2 Tbsp. unflavored gelatin (preferably vegetable based)
¾ cup pure apple juice
1½ cups scalding milk of choice
2 heaping Tbsp. Chicolin®/stevia mix
½ tsp. pumpkin pie spice
½ tsp. sea salt
3 cups cooked mashed pumpkin

Soak gelatin in first amount of juice for 1 minute. Add scalding milk. Blend until creamy. Add remaining ingredients. Blend all until smooth. Pour into a 9x9 square pan. Place in fridge and let set. Cut into bars and serve with a whipped topping from Bonus Collection.

Good summer dessert!

Creamy Topping

1¼ cups of vanilla rice milk
½ level cup light organic spelt flour
1 Tbsp. Chicolin®/stevia mix
½ cup grapeseed oil
1 tsp. vanilla extract

In a small pan, heat milk, flour and Chicolin™ mix. When thick, set aside to cool. Place this in a blender and slowly beat in the oil, then add vanilla. It's simple and easy. Good on puddings, homemade Jell-O pies and crisps.

58

Cool Cakes & Toppings Collection

This collection has great cakes and frostings that do not use icing sugar, dairy or wheat. The cakes are beneficial for those sufferers of allergies, Candida and Diabetes who cannot have regular cakes and frosting loaded with sugar. Taste for yourself.

It's about not giving up cake. It is about enjoying some on a special occasion too.

Give the recipe to a friend or family member, who will follow the recipe and come out with something presentable that will be satisfying and healthy. Now we can have a piece also. Enjoy!!

God's Blessings ~ Jeannine '2P' Edwards

Sunflower Apple Cake

1½ cups spelt flour
1 tsp. each of nutmeg, cinnamon and soda
½ tsp. sea salt
4 Tbsp. Chicolin®/stevia mix
¾ cup coconut oil or Better Butter **or** Earth Balance
2 beaten eggs or 4 Tbsp. Flax Gel
3 Granny Smith apples (grated)
½ cup sunflower seeds
1 tsp. vanilla extract

Preheat oven to 350°. Sift together all dry ingredients. Cream butter with eggs and add to dry ingredients. Add vanilla apples, and sunflower seeds. Bake for 45 minutes to 1 hour. Serve warm with cinnamon sauce.

Cinnamon Sauce

2 cups fresh apple juice
1 cup purified water
1/4 cup lemon juice
1/3 cup coconut oil **or** Better Butter **or** Earth Balance
1/3 cup spelt flour **or** tapioca starch
3 Tbsp. Chicolin®/stevia mix
1 tsp. cinnamon
1/8 tsp. nutmeg

In a saucepan over medium heat, combine all ingredients and mix well. Cook until thicken. Serve over warm cake. Rice Dream Ice cream goes well with this too.

Lemon Poppy Angel Cake

4 Tbsp. Chicolin®/stevia mix
¾ cup spelt flour
9 egg whites * Must use range free eggs; not replacer
½ tsp. cream of tartar
¼ tsp. sea salt
2 Tbsp. poppy seeds
1 tsp. lemon rind
1 tsp. vanilla extract

Preheat oven to 325º. Combine chicolin and flour in a bowl. Set aside. Beat the egg whites until they are very stiff adding the cream of tartar and the salt. Mix egg whites and flour together gently adding the poppy seeds, rind then vanilla. Pour into a greased tube cake pan bake 55 - 60 minutes. Remove from pan carefully and drizzle with Lemon Drizzle. Excellent! Chuck's favorite.

Lemon Drizzle

¾ cup fresh organic lemon juice
1 Tbsp. Chicolin®/stevia mix

Combine juice and chicolin mix in a saucepan. Bring to a boil Cool. Drizzle on cooled cake.

Cheating Chocolate Cake

2 Tbsp. Chicolin®/stevia mix
1¼ cups spelt flour
1/3 cup cocoa **or** carob
1½ tsp. soda
¾ tsp. homemade Baking Powder
Pinch of cinnamon
2 egg or 6 Tbsp. Flax Gel
¾ cup rice vanilla milk **or** goats **or** nut milk
2 tsp. lemon juice
¾ cup strong Café-Lib™
1/3 cup coconut oil **or** grapeseed oil

Preheat oven to 350º. Sift chicolin mix, flour, cocoa (or carob), soda, baking powder and cinnamon. Set aside. In a larger bowl, beat eggs, milk, lemon juice, coffee and oil. Add dry ingredients. Mix well. Pour into a square greased pan. Bake 30 minutes.

Cocoa or Carob Frosting

¼ cup cocoa **or** carob
2½ Tbsp. Chicolin®/stevia mix
8 tsp. tapioca **or** cornstarch
1 cup favorite milk

Using a double boiler or over hot water, combine all ingredients over medium heat. Stir frequently until thickened. Cool.

Sunflower Pumpkin Cake

¾ cup coconut oil **or** grapeseed oil **or** mixture of both
2 cups mashed pumpkin (best if you have homemade)
4 free range eggs **or** 12 Tbsp. Flax Gel
1½ tsp. almond extract
3 cups spelt flour
6 Tbsp. Chicolin®/stevia mix
2 tsp. soda
1 Tbsp. homemade Baking Powder
½ Tbsp. cinnamon
1 tsp. sea salt
1½ cups sunflower **or** pumpkin seeds

Preheat oven to 350°. In a bowl, mix oil, pumpkin, eggs and extract. In a separate bowl, combine all dry ingredients and set aside. Mix dry and wet ingredients together and add sunflower seeds. Pour evenly in 2 greased round pans and use wax paper in bottom. Bake 55 minutes. Cool and frost with butter frosting.

Butter Frosting

1 cup sunflower milk
4 Tbsp. organic light spelt flour **or** tapioca **or** arrowroot
½ cup Better Butter
½ cup coconut oil or Earth Balance Butter
2½ Tbsp. Chicolin®/stevia mix
2 tsp. vanilla extract

Mix together milk and flour. Cook stirring until thick. Cool. Cream together remaining ingredients. Beat until fluffy slowly adding milk/flour mixture. Best after a light meal.

Poppy Chiffon Cake

1 cup poppy seeds
1 cup purified water
2 cups spelt flour
4½ tsp. Chicolin®/stevia mix
1 tsp. sea salt
1 Tbsp. homemade Baking Powder
¼ tsp. baking soda
7 egg yolks
½ cup grapeseed oil
2 tsp. vanilla extract
7 egg whites beaten stiffly
2½ tsp. cream of tartar

The night before soak poppy seeds in water. Preheat oven to 325º. In a bowl, sift flour. Add all the remaining dry ingredients together. In a separate bowl, mix egg yolks with oil and vanilla. Pour into the dry ingredients with the water and poppy seeds. Mix well. In another bowl, add cream of tartar to stiff egg whites. Fold in the cake batter gently. Bake in greased tube pan 50 minutes increase heat to 350º and bake for 20-25 minutes longer.

USE BUTTER FROSTING FOR THIS CAKE ALSO (PREVIOUS RECIPE).

Light and Fluffy Sponge Cake

1 1/3 cups organic light spelt flour
2 tsp. homemade Baking Powder
¼ tsp. sea salt
3 Tbsp. Chicolin®/stevia mix
2 large organic eggs separated
½ tsp. each vanilla and lemon extracts
1/3 cup boiling water

Preheat oven to 325°. Mix and set aside flours, baking powder, salt and chicolin mix. Beat the egg whites until stiff. Beat the egg yolks adding the extracts and the boiling water. Whip really well. Beat the whites into the yolk mixture then add the flour slowly. When it is all mixed and the batter is light pour it into a greased angel food cakes pan. Bake the cake anywhere from 50 minutes to an hour.

Sugarless Orange Sauce

¾ cup orange juice
1 tsp. orange rind
1 tsp. corn **or** tapioca starch
1½ tsp. Chicolin®/stevia mix
1 tsp. Brandy extracts
2 Tbsp. coconut oil **or** Better Butter

Over hot water, in a saucepan mix the first 4 ingredients. Stir until thick. Add brandy and butter. Stir. Ready to serve.

Boston Cream Pie

5 Tbsp. coconut oil **or** Better Butter **or** Earth Balance
1 cup favorite milk (goat, rice, seed, soy or nut)
1 tsp. vanilla
3 tsp. Chicolin®/stevia mix
1¾ cups spelt flour
½ tsp. sea salt
2 tsp. homemade Baking Powder
2 egg whites * from free range

Preheat oven to 375º. In a bowl, mix butter, milk and vanilla. Meanwhile in a separate bowl, mix the remaining dry ingredients together. Mix the flour mixture into the milk mixture and beat until creamy. Set aside. Beat egg whites until stiff and gently add to cake mix. Beat well and pour into 2 round 8" greased pans. Bake 20 minutes.

Custard

1 cup favorite milk
3 Tbsp. tapioca starch
1½ tsp. Chicolin®/stevia mix
2 free range egg yolks
½ tsp. vanilla

Bring milk to a boil with the starch and chicolin mix. Continue to stir as it thickens. Add yolks and vanilla. Stir until thick and creamy. After cake has cooled, fill with this custard.

Topping

(FOR BOSTON CREAM PIE)

¼ cup cocoa **or** carob powder
2 tsp. Chicolin®/stevia mix
¼ cup purified water

Mix well. Drizzle frosting on top.

Jelly Roll

1¼ cups organic light spelt flour
1 tsp. homemade Baking Powder
½ tsp. sea salt
3 Tbsp. Chicolin®/stevia mix
5 free range eggs, separated
1 tsp. each lemon and orange extracts

Preheat oven to 400°. Mix the flours, baking powder, salt and Chicolin. In a separate bowl, beat yolks then add extracts. Fold flour mixture into yolks. In large bowl, whip egg whites. Add all to the whites. Grease 2 pans. Pour into pans. Bake 10 minutes. Cool. Remove from pans carefully using a T-towel. Fill with custard or fruit and roll Cut into slices.

Pineapple Upside Down Cake

I miss this cake. For those who can have pineapple, you will still be able to enjoy it without the brown sugar. This is as close as I can come to the original. Any fruit can be used such as peaches, pears, berries, apples, and cherries.

1 medium can drained cubed pineapple with juice
2 Tbsp Agave Nectar
1 Tbsp. Chicolin®/stevia mix
1 Tbsp. tapioca or arrowroot starch
¼ cup grapeseed oil
¼ cup coconut oil or Better Butter or Earth Balance Butter
1 well-beaten free range egg or 3 Tbsp. Flax Gel
¾ cup favorite milk
1 tsp. vanilla
2 Tbsp. Chicolin®/stevia mix
½ cup other flour (can be replaced with spelt or other)
1 cup of organic light spelt flour
2 tsp. homemade Baking Powder
½ tsp. sea salt

Preheat oven to 350°. In a 9x9-buttered pan, add a little agave nectar then arrange pineapple on bottom. Reserve juice. In a saucepan, bring the juice, 1 Tbsp. chicolin and starch to a boil. When it has thickened, pour over pineapple or keep it to glaze. In a bowl, combine oil, butter, egg, milk and vanilla. Add remaining ingredients together. Beat into a smooth batter and place over pineapple Bake 40 minutes. Serve warm with pineapple sauce.

Carrot Cake

2 cups light organic spelt flour
2 tsp. homemade Baking Powder
1½ tsp. each baking soda and cinnamon
5 Tbsp. Chicolin®/stevia mix
1 cup grapeseed oil **or** 2/3 cup coconut oil
3 free range eggs **or** 9 Tbsp. Flax Gel
2 cups grated carrots
2 cups drained crushed pineapple *opt
½ cup organic sunflower seeds
½ cup washed (no sculpture) raisins *opt not good for Candida

Preheat oven 350°. Sift flour; baking powder, soda, cinnamon & Chicolin mix together. Set aside. In a bowl combine the oil, beat in the eggs or flax gel, adding the carrots and pineapple and beat well. Add raisins if using and sunflower seeds to the flour mix. Beat in flour mix 1 cup at a time. Pour into a greased and floured 9x13 pan or 2 round 8" pans and bake 30 - 40 minutes inserting a toothpick to test. Cool. Optional: Carrot cake can be frosted with Butter frosting recipe found in the "Cool Cakes" section (look in the index, in the back of the book for the recipe).

Cookies and Delectable Dessert Squares Collection

Make cookies for your small kids and the large kids too. This variety should be ample and delightful for those who are not allowed sugar, milk or dairy.

I offer you recipes free from sugar, dairy and white and whole-wheat flour. Not to say, that you cannot make them with these ingredients but because you have difficulties with some of these ingredients you may use what is for you. Any ingredient may be replaced. Everything is interchangeable.

A cookie was once called a small cake or a biscuit. The Dutch actually named the cookie derived from the word "Koekje" or "Koekie" meaning a small cake.

The Americans actually named it the cookie and the English the biscuit.

There are so many varieties of cookies, because of shapes, sizes and flavor. Bars and squares, drop cookies, rolled cookies, pressed cookies, and molded cookies.

Bars and drops are made with more liquids. Some are a stiffer dough, which is less sweet and fatter.

Cookie dough may be stored in the refrigerator. Most may be frozen up to 6 months.

Bars can be stored in baking pans covered; soft cookies can be stored in airtight containers in a cool place.

To re-crisp place on cookie sheet for 5 minutes

Crunchies

Base:

1½ sticks of Earth Balance Butter **or** ¾ cup Better Butter
2 egg yolks
3Tbsp. Chicolin®/stevia mix
2½ cups organic spelt flour **or** other
Pinch sea salt

Top:

4 Tbsp. Chicolin®/stevia mix
½ cup agave nectar
1 stick (½ cup) Health Balance Butter
1/3 cup sunflower seeds
1/3 cup water to make cream
1 cup each sesame seeds **and** sunflower seeds

Preheat oven to 350°. Cream butter and eggs. Add the dry ingredients of chicolin mix, flour and salt. Mix well. Press unto a greased or lined cookie sheet. Bake 15-20 minutes.

Meanwhile, in a blender add the 1/3 cup sunflower seeds. Add water to make a heavy cream. Set aside.
Heat the chicolin mix, agave nectar and butter in a small saucepan and bring to a boil. Boil 5 minutes and stir until chicolin has dissolved. Stir in the nut cream and the nuts. Pour over the base and spread evenly. Bake another 20 minutes until brown. Cool and cut.

Dutch Squares

1 tsp. almond extract
1 free range beaten egg or replacer
½ cup coconut oil **or** Better Butter **or** Earth Balance Butter
1½ cup light organic spelt flour
3 Tbsp. Chicolin®/stevia mix
½ tsp. homemade Baking Powder
1 free range egg or replacer
1 Tbsp. vanilla rice milk
½ cup sliced almonds or other such as sunflower seeds for those who cannot have nuts.

Preheat oven 350º. In a bowl add the extract, egg and butter. Cream these together. Add the spelt, Chicolin mix and baking powder. Pat in a greased 9x9 square pan for thicker or in a 9x13 pan for a thinner square. Beat the egg and milk together. Brush the top of the square. Sprinkle the nuts on top of the square and bake 30 minutes.

Coconut Macaroons

2 free range egg whites beaten stiff
1/8 tsp. sea salt
1/8 tsp. cream of tartar
¼ tsp. Chicolin®/stevia mix
½ tsp. vanilla **or** almond extract
2/3 cups unsweetened coconut

Preheat oven to 325º. Beat egg whites until very stiff add the salt, cream of tartar, Chicolin mix and extract. Fold in the coconut.

Drop by Tbsp. on greased cookie sheet. Bake slowly for 20 minutes.

Fruit Jam Filled Cookies

2 well beaten free range eggs **or** 2 Tbsp. Flax Gel **or** replacer
½ cup coconut oil **or** vegetable shortening **or** grapeseed oil
3 Tbsp. Chicolin®/stevia + ½ tsp. nutmeg
2 cups of light organic spelt **or** other flour
2 tsp. homemade Baking Powder
Home made fruit jams (raspberry or other)

Preheat oven to 350°. Beat the eggs or replacer with the shortening or oil. Mix the Chicolin mix with the flour, baking powder and nutmeg and add it to the egg mixture. Make dough but DO NOT OVERWORK it. Add more flour if you need it to make nice manageable dough. Roll out and cut into 24 rounds. Cover one with the jam and cover with another round. Make a hole in the center so that the steam will escape and not lose its cover. Bake 15 minutes.

No Egg Sesame Thimble Cookies

3 cups spelt flour + ¼ cup grounded sunflower seeds
½ cup sesame seeds + ½ tsp. sea salt
2½ Tbsp. Chicolin®/stevia mix
1½ sticks of Earth Balance Butter
4 tsp. pure vanilla + ¼ tsp. almond extracts

Preheat oven to 350°. Mix flour, sunflower seeds, salt and chicolin mix in a large bowl. Make a well and add butter and extracts. Mix until well blended. Add the sesame seeds. Roll into small balls and make an imprint with your thumb in the center. Place on cookie sheets and chill. Bake 10 minutes.

Half of the dough can be used the other half frozen or made into crescent rolls and bake 10 min. Roll in plain chicolin. Before the thimbles cool and fill with unsweetened jam or make into crescent rolls. These cookies are a great luncheon and tea time favorite!

Swirls

2 cups spelt flour + 2½ Tbsp. Chicolin®/stevia mix
¼ tsp. sea salt + 1 tsp. homemade Baking Powder
1/3 cup sunflower seeds
1½ sticks of Earth Balance Butter
1 beaten free range egg
1 tsp. vanilla extract
½ cup unsweetened raspberry jam

Preheat oven to 350º. Mix flour, chicolin mix, salt and baking powder. In a large bowl, cream butter, egg and vanilla. Mix flour mixture into egg mixture and beat. Chill the dough. Divide in 2 and rolled each. Spread with ¼ cup of jam and crushed sunflower seeds, then rolled like jelly roll and slice. Bake 15 minutes.

 May be frozen.

Tropical Squares

1/3 cup each chopped dates, raisins **and** figs **or** 1 cup of either
2 small cans crushed drained pineapple
½ cup purified water
¾ tsp. vanilla extract
1½ cups light organic spelt flour
1½ cups spelt flakes (whirl in blender for a few minutes)
1 cup coconut oil **or** Better Butter **or** Earth Balance
½ cup coconut **or** sunflower seeds

Preheat oven to 350º. Cook the dates, raisins, figs and pineapple in the purified water until soft and add vanilla. Mix the flour and the flakes cutting in the butter. Add the coconut or seeds. Place 1/2 the mix in a square 9x9 pan and cover with the filling, then add rest of mixture. Bake 30 minutes.

Carob or Chocolate Brownies

2 squares unsweetened chocolate /**or** 2 cups chocolate /**or** carob chips /**or** 4 Tbsp. cocoa and 3 Tbsp. butter
1/3 cup coconut oil or Earth Balance Butter
1/3 cup unsweetened applesauce
2 free-range eggs **or** replacer
½ tsp. vanilla extract
½ cup light organic spelt flour
5 Tbsp. Chicolin®/stevia
1/8 tsp. sea salt
1 cup chopped walnuts **or** sunflower seeds

Preheat oven to 350º. Over hot water, melt chocolate (or carob) with butter. Stir until creamy. Set aside. Beat the eggs or replacer, stir in vanilla, chocolate or carob mixture. Fold in flour, chicolin, salt, nuts or seeds. Spread in greased 8x8 pan. Bake 12 minutes. Cool. Cut in squares.

Icing:
3 squares of dark unsweetened chocolate **or** 9 Tbsp. carob **or** 5 Tbsp. cocoa your choice
6 Tbsp. Chicolin mix **or** 6 Tbsp. agave nectar for sweeter
2/3 cup milk.
½ tsp. vanilla extract
3 Tbsp. Better Butter

Mix and cook first 3 ingredients over hot water until form softball in cold water. Beat in vanilla and Better Butter.

If you have any left over place in small container and cool. Just like chocolate fudge.

Egg-less No Bake Apricot Coconut Balls

(This recipe is not for those who have Candida; it is good for people on a "Raw Foods" Diet)

1 cup dried apricots
1½ cups unsweetened coconut
½ cup dried oranges
¾ cups sunflower seeds
½ cup raisins
3 Tbsp. lemon juice
1 Tbsp. orange peel

Cover all the fruit overnight with the lemon juice. Grind it well adding the seeds and peel. Roll into balls then into coconut.

Egg-less No Bake Carob Peanut Clusters

For Candida replace peanuts with sunflower seeds
3 Tbsp. carob **or** cocoa
1/3 cup rice vanilla milk
Bring to a boil and add
butter 1cup spelt flakes
  ½ cup peanuts or sunflower seeds

3 tbsp. Chicolin®/stevia mix
¼ cup Earth Balance Butter
¼ cup peanut butter **or** seed

Drop unto wax paper.

Egg-less Christmas Carob Clusters

3 Tbsp. carob powder
1 cup spelt flakes browned in oven
½ stick (¼ cup) Earth Balance Butter
1/3 cup rice vanilla milk
3 Tbsp. Chicolin®/stevia mix
¼ cup peanut or nut butter
½ cup seeds or nuts

Over hot water in a pot place the carob, butter and milk. Bring to a boil & add the nut butter. In a large bowl place the spelt flakes and pour the carob mix on top of it. Add the nuts or seeds and drop on wax paper into clusters.

Egg-less No Bake Chocolate or Carob Crispies

1½ cups dark unsweetened chocolate **or** 1½ cups dark no sugar chocolate wafers **or** 1½ cups carob chips (no sugar)
1/3 cup Earth Balance Butter
2 cups puffed rice
½ cup nuts **or** seeds
¼ cup white sugar free white chocolate wafers

Line a 9x9 pan with parchment paper. Melt carob or chocolate & butter. Add puffs & half the nuts or seeds. Press down into pan then press in the rest of the nuts or seeds. Drizzle white chocolate if using chocolate on top. Chill cut into fingers. Good for celiac.

Egg-less No Bake Rice Choco or Carob Drops

2 cups sugarless chocolate wafers **or** carob chips
2 cups Kamut **or** rice cereal
1 cup unsweetened coconut

Melt chocolate or carob, add cereal and add coconut. Drop on wax paper and chill. Good for celiac.

No Bake Vegan Sunflower Seed Balls

2 Tbsp. Earth Balance Butter
3 Tbsp. Chicolin®/stevia mix
1 cup sunflower seed butter
1 cup unsweetened coconut
1 cup chopped sunflower seeds

Make into balls and roll into coconut. Good for allergies, candida, celiac and diabetics.

Eggless Carob/Chocolate Drop Cookies

1 stick (½ cup) Earth Balance Butter
½ cup vanilla rice milk
Tbsp. Chicolin®/stevia mix
½ cup carob or cocoa
2 ½ cups of filler such as dried fruit, nuts and/or seeds, coconut, spelt flakes, whatever you have.
(Let your imagination soar when looking for additional ingredients; use up your leftovers in the cupboard).

Preheat oven to 350°. Mix together in a bowl. Drop by rounded tsp. on a lined cookie sheet. Bake 12-15 minutes.

Egg-less No Bake Peanut Balls

Use the same recipe as eggless carob/chocolate drop cookies (above) using ½ cup peanuts.

Egg-less Crunchy Chocolate or Carob Balls

2¼ cups spelt flour **or** other flours
7 Tbsp. Earth Balance Butter
6 Tbsp. Chicolin®/stevia mix
1½ tsp. vanilla extract
Pinch homemade Baking Powder
1 cup cocoa **or** carob

Preheat oven to 350°. Mix the dry ingredients and make a well in the center. Add butter, milk and vanilla. Mix well. Make into a log. Chill 2 to 6 hours. Cut and bake 15 minutes.

Egg-less Poppy Seed Squares

1½ cups spelt flour
½ cup Earth Balance butter
4½ Tbsp. Chicolin®/stevia mix
1/3 cup agave nectar
1 tsp. homemade Baking Powder
2 Tbsp. vanilla rice milk
¼ tsp. baking soda
½ tsp. vanilla extract
½ tsp. sea salt
¼ tsp. almond extract
1/3 cup poppy seeds
1 cup unsweetened coconut

Preheat oven to 350º. Combine dry ingredients except coconut & seeds. Cream butter, agave, milk & extracts. Mix well & add dry ingredients. Beat well; add coconut & poppy seeds. Spread into 9x13 pan &bake 30 mins. Drizzle with carob or chocolate.

Egg-less Filled Cookies

1½ cups spelt flour
1/3 cup Earth Balance Butter
½ tsp. each soda, nutmeg, cinnamon and ginger
1 tsp. vanilla extract and orange peel
Pinch cloves
1½ Tbsp. Chicolin®/stevia mix
½ cup each raisins and sunflower seeds
tsp. marmalade (no sugar brand) in thumbprint of each cookie (1 batch usually yields ½ jar of marmalade)

Preheat oven to 350º. Mix dry ingredients & peel. Set aside. Cream butter; add vanilla. Add flour mix with raisins & chopped seeds. Roll into balls. Make thumbprints. Bake 10 mins. Cool & fill with marmalade.

Raisins Molasses Treasures

¾ cup Earth Balance Shortening
¼ cup blackstrap molasses
1 free range egg
¼ cup vanilla rice milk
1 cup washed raisins
2 cups spelt
3 Tbsp. Chicolin®/stevia mix
1 tsp. cinnamon
½ tsp. each cloves and ginger
Pinch sea salt

Preheat oven to 350º. Mix dry ingredients. Set aside. Cream shortening, molasses, egg & milk. Add dry ingredients. Mix well. Add raisins & chill overnight. Make into 1" balls & place on cookie sheet 2" apart. Bake 10 minutes.

Sunflower Macaroons

2 cups coconut
2½ Tbsp. Chicolin®/stevia mix
¼ cup spelt flour
¼ tsp. sea salt
1 beaten egg whites (beaten)
1½ cups chopped sunflower seeds
¼ cup finely cut dried fruit
1 tsp. vanilla extract

Preheat oven to 325º. Mix chicolin mix, coconut, spelt flour and salt. Beat egg white until foamy adding vanilla & dry ingredients then chopped sunflower seeds or nuts and dried fruit. Drop on greased cookie sheet and bake for 25 minutes.

Surprise Bites

1 cup finely chopped dates
1 cup finely chopped sunflower seeds
2½ tsp. lemon juice
1 stick of Earth Balance Butter
2 well beaten free range eggs
1½ Tbsp. Chicolin®/stevia mix
2 cups spelt flour
1 tsp. homemade Baking Powder
Chicolin no Stevia

Preheat oven to 350º. Mix dates & seeds & sprinkle lemon juice on top. Set aside. Cream butter & eggs. Mix dry ingredients & add to butter mix. Make the fruit mix into small balls & take a bit of dough & wrap around the fruit balls. Roll into chicolin. Bake 15 minutes. The chicolin makes the balls glisten.

Snowy Brownie Cookie

½ cup Earth Balance Butter
2 free range eggs
1 tsp. vanilla extract
1 cup dark sugarless chocolate wafers or carob chips, melted
¾ Tbsp. Chicolin®/stevia mix
1 cup spelt flakes
¾ cup spelt flour
1 tsp. homemade Baking Powder
¾ Chicolin®/stevia mix
¾ white sugarless chocolate wafers

Preheat oven to 350º. Mix butter, eggs and melted wafers. Beat. Mix spelt flakes, flour, baking powder and chicolin mix together. Add to butter mixture then add the white wafers and drop by Tbsp on **ungreased** cookie sheet. Bake 10 minutes. For all you brownie lovers, this one's a hit!

Lebkuchen

¼ Tbsp. Chicolin®/stevia mix
1 Tbsp. Earth Balance Butter
¾ cup agave nectar
½ tsp. each sea salt, soda, cinnamon and allspice
1 free range egg
3 Tbsp. orange rind
1½ cups spelt flour
1 tsp. each nutmeg and ginger
¾ cup sunflower seeds
¾ cup dried fruit

Preheat oven to 350º. In small saucepan, melt butter with chicolin mix and agave nectar. DO NOT BOIL. Cool and pour in large bowl adding the egg and orange rind. Mix the dry ingredients together adding them in turn with the fruit and seeds to the butter mixture. Cover and set bowl in fridge for 4 days. Divide the dough and cut into bars and bake 10 mins. Cool and glaze. Good Christmas bars.

Coconut Cherry Circles

1 stick of Earth Balance Butter
1½ cups spelt flour
1 free range egg
½ Tbsp. Chicolin®/stevia mix
3 Tbsp. vanilla rice milk
Toasted unsweetened coconut

Preheat oven to 375º. With beater, cream butter adding half the flour adding egg, vanilla & milk. Add the rest, whipping it then the coconut. Drop by tsp. on cookie sheet. Bake 10 minutes then cool. **Glaze**: 6 Tbsp. chicolin mix with a little cherry juice (approximately 1 tsp. of the juice).

Lemon Snaps

1 stick of Earth Balance Butter
1 free range egg
1 tsp. vanilla extract
2 tsp. lemon rind
1½ tsp. lemon juice
1 Tbsp. Chicolin®/stevia mix
1 tsp. homemade Baking Powder
1¾ cups spelt flour

Preheat oven to 350º. Beat egg, vanilla and lemon rind. Mix all the dry ingredients together. Mix the wet and the dry together. Set in plastic bag in fridge for 1 hour to a day or more then roll out and cut with cookie cutters, bake 15 minutes, cool and ice.

Christmas Deco Cookies

1 stick Earth Balance Butter
2 free range eggs
1½ tsp. vanilla
1 Tbsp. Chicolin/stevia mix
1/3 cup spelt flour
1 cup spelt flakes
1½ tsp. homemade Baking Powder
½ tsp. sea salt

Preheat oven to 375º. Cream butter, eggs & vanilla. Mix chicolin mix, flour, flakes, baking powder & salt and add to butter mixture. Work dough into a ball & chill overnight. Roll out cookie dough and cut with cutters. Bake 10 minutes.
Glaze: 6 Tbsp. Chicolin®/stevia mix and ½ tsp. vanilla extract. Adding a little vanilla rice milk until right consistency.

Carob or Chocolate Berry Bar

1/3 cup Earth Balance Butter
¼ cup carob **or** cocoa
1 free range egg
½ tsp. vanilla extract
¾ cup spelt flour
¼ tsp. soda
¼ tsp. homemade Baking Powder
½ Tbsp. Chicolin®/stevia mix
1/3 cup homemade sugarless raspberry jam

Preheat oven to 350º. Mix and set aside flour, soda, baking powder and chicolin mix. Melt butter, cocoa or carob; add vanilla and egg. Beat then add milk. Beat in the flour mix. Spread in a 9x9 square pan. Bake 25 mins. Let cool. Spread jam on top.

Drizzle: ¼ cup carob or cocoa, 2 tsp. Chicolin®/stevia mix, ¼ cup water. Mix together & drizzle over top bars.

Sesame Cookies

¾ cup Earth Balance Butter
2 beaten free range eggs
4 Tbsp. sesame seeds
½ cup spelt flour
1 Tbsp. Chicolin®/stevia mix
1 Tbsp. homemade Baking Powder
¾ cup Rice milk
3-5 tsp. Sesame seeds (add according to your taste)

Preheat oven to 350º. Cream butter, half the flour, eggs and sesame seeds. Mix balance of flour in with the Chicolin added, baking powder. Blend this all well with the first batter. Chill overnight. Roll and cut with fancy cutters then brush with milk and sprinkle with sesame seeds. Bake 10 minutes.

Holiday Bars

2 cups spelt flour
1 tsp. cinnamon
½ tsp. each nutmeg and ginger
1/3 tsp. soda
¼ tsp. each allspice and cloves
½ cup Earth Balance Butter
1 free range egg
¾ cup rice vanilla milk + 1 tsp. lemon juice
1/3 cup blackstrap molasses
½ cup chopped sunflower seeds
2/3 cups dried fruit (not glazed) soaked in an unsweetened juice

Preheat oven to 350º. Grease a 10x15x1 pan. Mix all the dry ingredients together. Set aside. Cream the butter, egg, vanilla, and molasses. Beat in the flour mix and seeds and fruit. Spread on the greased sheet. Bake 15-20 minutes, ice and decorate with cherries (don't eat them). **Icing**: With 6 Tbsp. Chicolin, mix 1 tsp. orange juice. You may have to add more juice according to the consistency.

Spritz Cookies

3 sticks or 1½ cups Earth Balance Butter
½ tsp. almond extract
1 tsp. vanilla extract
1 free range egg
3 Tbsp. Chicolin®/stevia mix
2½ cups spelt flour
1 tsp. homemade Baking Powder

Preheat oven to 375º. Mix the 2½ cups spelt with baking powder. Set aside. In large bowl beat butter, extracts & egg. Add flour; makes a soft dough, press through cookie press. To make carob or cocoa remove 6 Tbsp. of flour and add 6 Tbsp. carob or cocoa. Bake 10 mins. DO NOT CHILL.

Snow Flakes

2 cups spelt flour
1½ tsp. homemade Baking Powder
¼ tsp. each sea salt and nutmeg
½ tsp. cinnamon
2½ Tbsp. Chicolin®/stevia mix
½ cup Earth Balance Butter + ½ stick Earth Balance Shortening
1 Tbsp. lemon juice
1 free range egg

Preheat oven to 375º. Sift all dry ingredients together. Set aside. Cream butter & shortening, juice & egg. Beat in flour; chill overnight. Roll out & cut with scalloped round cutter. Poke holes in cookie with straw. Bake 10 mins, cool & dust with Chicolin®.

Biscotti

3 cups spelt flour
2½ tsp. homemade Baking Powder
3 Tbsp. Chicolin®/stevia mix
1 stick Earth Balance Butter
2 free range eggs + 1 egg yolk
¼ tsp. crushed anise
2 Tbsp. orange peel
1 tsp. water + 1 egg white
1cup finely chopped mixed fruit (not for Candida; use seeds)

Preheat oven to 350º. Sift 2 cups flour, baking powder & 3 T chicolin mix. Cream butter, egg, yolk, & anise & remaining flour. Beat add orange peel. Add fruit. Make into 2 loaves. Sprinkle with Chicolin brush with water & egg wash. Bake 25 mins. Cool; slice bake 10 min. then turn and bake 15 mins. Dust with Chicolin®. (no stevia – just like above recipe)

Very Berry Square

1¼ cup light organic spelt flour
½ tsp. sea salt
½ tsp. Chicolin®/stevia
1 tsp. homemade baking powder
½ cup coconut oil or better butter or Earth Balance
1 free range egg yolk or 3. Tbsp. Flax Gel
2 Tbsp. favorite milk (goat **or** rice **or** nut)
¾ cup favorite homemade berry jam
2 tsp. vanilla extract
7 Tbsp. coconut oil **or** Better Butter **or** Earth Balance Butter
4 Tbsp. Chicolin®/stevia mix
2½ cups unsweetened coconut
2 eggs beaten **or** egg replacer

Preheat oven 350º. Mix flour, salt, and Chicolin mix baking powder. Cut in ½ cup butter, 1 egg yolk and milk. Pat in a 9x9 or 9x13 greased square pan. Spread the jam over the top. Set aside. Beat the eggs, vanilla, butter, Chicolin mix and the coconut. Pour over the jam layer and bake for 35 minutes.

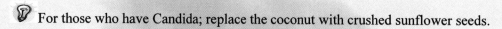 For those who have Candida; replace the coconut with crushed sunflower seeds.

Pineapple Squares

½ cup coconut oil **or** Better Butter **or** Earth Balance
1¼ cup light organic spelt
¾ Tbsp. Chicolin®/stevia mix
2 free-range eggs **or** replacer
1 cup crushed drained pineapple
½ tsp. almond extract
2 Tbsp. Chicolin®/stevia mix
½ tsp. homemade Baking Powder
¼ tsp. sea salt
2 Tbsp. light organic spelt flour or other
½ cup nuts **or** seeds

Preheat 350°. Mix the ½ cup butter with flour and chicolin mix. Pat in a square 9x9 pan or 9x13 for daintier squares. Bake 12 minutes. Cool. Beat the eggs, adding pineapple & extract. In the same bowl, mix the dry ingredients of chicolin, baking powder, salt & flour. Add the seeds or nuts. Pour on the top of cooked crust and bake 25 -30 minutes. Then ice with following recipe.

Icing for Pineapple Squares

3 level Tbsp. Chicolin®/stevia mix
2 Tbsp. Better Butter **or** coconut oil **or** Earth Balance
½ cup crushed pineapple
3 Tbsp. tapioca flour **or** arrowroot **or** cornstarch.

Cook over hot water. Add more juice if needed.

Coconut Bars

½ cup coconut oil **or** soft Better Butter **or** Earth Balance
2 Tbsp. Chicolin®/stevia mix
1¼ cup light organic spelt flour or other or mix
2 free range eggs
½ tsp. sea salt
1 tsp. vanilla extract
1½ cups coconut
1 cup chopped nuts **or** sunflower seeds
¼ cup light organic spelt flour **or** other
3 Tbsp. Chicolin®/stevia mix

Preheat the oven to 375°. Beat the butter and add first amount of Chicolin with the flour. Pat in a 9x13 square greased pan for thinner crust or 9x9 for thicker crust. Bake 12 minutes. Beat eggs. Add salt, vanilla and coconut and nuts or seeds. Add the flour and second amount of Chicolin mix. Pour over the cooked crust. Bake for 20 minutes.

Lemon Cookies

1 stick of Earth Balance Butter **or** ½ cup of coconut oil **or** ½ cup Better Butter
1 free range egg
2 tsp. lemon rind **or** peel
1½ tsp. fresh organic lemon juice
3 Tbsp. Chicolin®/stevia mix
1 tsp. homemade Baking Powder
1¾ cups of spelt organic flour

Heat oven to 350°. In a large bowl beat the butter and eggs adding the rind or peel and lemon juice. In a separate bowl, add dry ingredients and mix. Add flour mixture to wet ingredients. Mix dough and place in the refrigerator overnight or several hours. This can be frozen for several months at this time. You may divide it and use one portion at a time. Roll out the dough and cut with favorite cutter and bake 15 minutes. Cool and ice with either frostings.

Melt white chocolate wafers (no sugar) or 6 Tbsp. plain Chicolin®, ¼ tsp. butter of choice, a drop or two of lemon juice and Agave Nectar.

I have found the icing nicer combining agave nectar and chicolin than with using chicolin and stevia.

Mmmmm…..

~Just like Gramma used to make~

Plentiful Pies Collection

You will find flaky fruit pies as well as cream pies. Not to worry, they are made as healthy as you can possibly make a pie.

They are low fat, no sugar, and no dairy and made with organic healthy spelt flour or that of your choice. If you decide to serve them I know they will be enjoyed, especially with Rice Dream Ice cream™.

I use Earth Balance natural shortening. It is wonderful has no cholesterol, low in sodium, No gluten, dairy or egg. Made from exceller pressed natural oils of palm fruit, soybean, canola seed and olive. They are non-G.M.O it is patented balanced of fats to improve cholesterol; it has no Trans fatty acids and is non-hydrogenated.

Thanks, to my friend, **Elsie Swartz**. She made me aware of this product and I have used it in my cooking class and have produced satisfactory results. *It leaves the pastry easy to roll and is very flaky. You will find it satisfactory.* Give friends and family a call and invite them over for pie everyone can enjoy. I use Earth Balance shortening with zero (0%) cholesterol.

Some of the recipes call for a **baked pie shell**.

Preheat oven to 375°. Line pie plate with pastry and bake up to 10 minutes. Watch carefully! It may burn easily

Taste and performance superb!
Million thanks, Elsie

Spelt Pie Crust

(Makes 2 pies; bottom and top crusts)

2½ cups light organic spelt flour
Pinch sea salt
¾ cup Earth Balance vegetable shortening **or** 2/3 cup coconut oil
½ cup ice cold water

Mix flour and salt .Cut in shortening. Add water. Mix gently.

Overworking will result in a tough pastry. Make your pies at night and keep in the fridge, better still make and freeze. Cook frozen, they will be flakier.

Pie Crust

4 cups organic spelt flour
1 tsp. sea salt
1½ cups of coconut oil butter
1 cup iced purified water
2 tsp. Omega Apple Cider (I would use lemon juice)

Mix the dry ingredients. Cut in Coconut butter until it is crumbly. Add vinegar (or lemon juice) to water. Mix and add more if needed. Refrigerate 1 hour. Roll and use. Keeps 1 week in refrigerator. Makes 2 double pies.

No Cook Berry Pie

1 cooked spelt pie shell
2 cups of fresh berries
2 Tbsp. clear gel in a little warm water
½ tsp. Chicolin®/stevia
2 Tbsp. grapeseed oil
3 cups of berries (for top)
2 tsp. Chicolin®/stevia

Blend the 2 cups of berries, gel, 1 tsp. chicolin and oil. Place ½ mixture in bottom of pie crust. Place the 1½ cups of sliced berries over, dust with chicolin. Place the remaining gel filling on top of the pie. Add a layer of sweet berries. Dust again with chicolin mix. So good!

Cherry Peach Pie

1 Tbsp. Chicolin®/stevia mix
1/3 cup spelt organic light flour
1 cup drained cherries (from home canning.)
¼ cup of cherry juice
2 cups peaches sliced (from home canning)
¼ tsp. almond extract
3 Tbsp. Better Butter **or** Earth Balance

Preheat oven to 400°. Mix chicolin mix and flour together. Sprinkle 1/3 of flour mixture on bottom of unbaked pie shell. Add fruit. Combine extract and cherry juice together. Pour over fruit in pie. Sprinkle the rest of the flour over the fruit. Add butter. Cover with pastry. Bake for 40 - 50 minutes. Mmm good!!

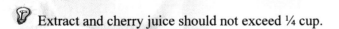 Extract and cherry juice should not exceed ¼ cup.

Aunt Mae's Pumpkin Pie

3 free range beaten eggs
1½ cups pumpkin (best if fresh)
3 Tbsp.Chicolin® /stevia mix + 2 tsp.
1 tsp. ginger
½ tsp. cinnamon
½ tsp. clove
14-oz goat's milk or nut milk

Preheat oven to 425°F. Combine all ingredients and fill unbaked pie shell. Bake 30 – 45 minutes

Goat's milk will result in a richer pie! Still good with other milk.

Egg Nog Custard Pie

3 beaten egg yolks from free range chickens
1½ Tbsp. Chicolin® /stevia mix
2 cups goat's milk, soy, rice **or** nut milk
½ tsp. vanilla
Dash sea salt
Dash nutmeg
3 free range beaten egg whites

Preheat oven to 400°F. Combine first 6 ingredients together. In a separate bowl, beat egg whites until stiff and fold into milk/egg mixture. Pour into unbaked pie shell. Bake 25 – 30 minutes.

Lemon Mousse Pie

3 free range eggs
¼ cup Better Butter **or** coconut oil **or** Earth Balance
3 Tbsp. Chicolin® /stevia mix
3½ Tbsp. light organic spelt flour
4 Tbsp. fresh lemon juice
2 tsp. grated lemon rind from organic lemons
½ cup milk (goat, soy, nut **or** rice)

Preheat oven to 450°. Separate eggs. Beat egg whites. Set aside. Mix butter, chicolin mix and flour. Beat egg yolks and add remaining ingredients. Fold in egg whites. Pour into a 9" unbaked pie shell Bake 8 minutes then lower temperature to 325° for 30 minutes.

Cranberry Apple Pie

2 packages of raw cleaned cranberries
3 large green (Granny Smith) apples, grated
½ cup purified water
2½ Tbsp. Chicolin ®/stevia mix
2 Tbsp. each organic spelt flour and tapioca starch
1/8 tsp. sea salt
2 Tbsp. Better Butter **or** Earth Balance

Heat oven to 375°. Cook cranberries in water about 10 mins, add apples, chicolin mix, flour, starch and salt. Cool. Fill unbaked pie shell. Dot with butter, cover with top crust and bake 30–35 minutes.

 If celiac use all tapioca starch instead of mix with spelt flour.

Blueberry Peach or Pear Pie

3 cups sliced peaches or pear
3½ cups Chicolin® /stevia mix+2 Tbsp.
1/3 cup spelt flour **or** tapioca starch
1 tsp. organic fresh lemon juice
1 tsp. lemon zest
3 cups blueberries

Preheat oven to 375°. Bring all ingredients except blueberries to a boil. Cool. Add blueberries. Pour into an unbaked pie shell. Cover with top pastry crust & chill. Egg wash with 1 beaten egg and 2 T water Bake for 35 - 40 mins. In a saucepan, combine chicolin mix, cornstarch & milk. Cook until thick stirring frequently. Remove some & add beaten eggs. Return to saucepan. Stir in ginger. Cook 2 mins. Stir in vanilla. Pour into baked pie shell. Cool & chill.

Pineapple Pie

2 cups pineapple juice
3 heaping Tbsp. Chicolin® /stevia mix
1/3 cup cornstarch **or** tapioca starch
3 free range beaten egg yolks (organic)
1½ cups pineapple chunks
1 Tbsp. Better Butter **or** Earth Balance
¼ tsp. sea salt
2 egg whites (organic)
¼ tsp. cream of tartar
½ tsp. Chicolin® /stevia mix

Preheat oven to 350°. Heat juice to boiling point. Combine with next 4 ingredients in double boiler & cook 12 mins until thick. Boil 3 mins. Remove from stove & add butter & salt. Cool mixture. Pour into cool baked pie shell.

Beat egg whites, cream of tartar & chicolin mix to form meringue. Spread over pie Brown in oven for 15 – 20 mins or until golden brown.

Lemon Pie

3 heaping Tbsp. Chicolin® /stevia mix + 1/2 tsp.
1/3 cup cornstarch **or** tapioca starch
2 cups boiling water (purified)
3 free range beaten egg yolks (organic)
1 tsp. grated lemon rind (organic)
½ cup fresh lemon juice
1 Tbsp. Better butter **or** Earth Balance
¼ tsp. sea salt
1 baked pie shell
2 egg whites (organic)
¼ tsp. cream of tartar
½ tsp. Chicolin® /stevia mix

Preheat oven to 350°. Combine first 5 ingredients in a double boiler and cook 12 minutes until thick. Boil 3 minutes. Remove from stove and add lemon juice, butter and salt. Cool mixture. Pour into cool baked pie shell.

Beat egg whites with cream of tartar and chicolin mix to form a meringue. Spread over lemon pie. Brown in oven for 15 to 20 minutes or until golden brown.

Fruit Pie

3 or 3 ¼ cups fresh fruit, washed and slice if necessary

🍐 To determine how much fruit you need, place fruit in empty pie plate you will be using until very full.

3 Tbsp. Chicolin®/stevia mix

1/3 cup light organic spelt flour **or** 3 Tbsp. tapioca

¼ tsp. sea salt

1 tsp. organic fresh lemon juice

Preheat oven to 375°. In a large bowl add fruit, chicolin mix, flour, salt and lemon juice. Fill the uncooked pie shell with fruit mix and dot with butter. Cover with top layer of pastry. Brush a milk-wash over the crust with your favorite milk. Prick to let out steam. Bake for 35 - 40 minutes. Tip; (It may be better to toss fruit with flour then sprinkle chicolin mix on fruit in pie in layers.

Cream Pie

2½ Tbsp. Chicolin®/stevia mix

7 Tbsp. light organic spelt flour **or** 9 Tbsp. tapioca starch

2 free range egg yolks

3 cups favorite milk (rice, nut, soy, goat, seed)

1 tsp. vanilla

1 baked pie shell

1 Tbsp. Better Butter

2 egg whites +1/2 tsp. Chicolin®/stevia mix

1/8 tsp. cream of tartar + ½ tsp. vanilla extract

Choice of banana, coconut, peach or pineapple

Preheat oven to 350°. Combine the chicolin mix, flour and milk in a saucepan. Cook until thick. Add egg yolks and butter. Beat egg whites with the chicolin, cream of tartar and vanilla. Place the fruit on the bottom crust and fill with the filling then a row of fruit and the meringue. Bake 15 minutes. Chill.

Now you can have your cake and eat it too...

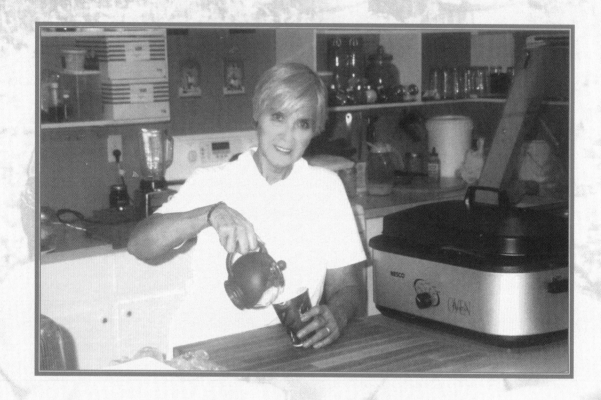

Without the Sugar!

Dessert by Dezine Collection

This Collection offers you a selection of light desserts to tickle your palate. It will serve you well in the hot summer months and after a meal when you're looking for that little something extra. Everything offered in these recipes are made with no dairy, sugar, and wheat and delightful desserts. Making meals 3 times a day 7 days a week is a full time job. Even if you love cooking, it takes a lot of time and energy. Don't you find having to think of something to make is sometimes more of a task than making it?

There are pies, muffins, cookies, squares and cakes that we have introduced but sometimes a pudding or sherbet is a nice change .A light dessert after a heavy meal hits the spot.

Desserts by Dezine have such recipes that will be light and enjoyable in the summer or at any time. Feel free to add to these recipes should something not be to your liking. These recipes can be adjusted according to your taste and your needs. You will find sherbet, puddings, freezes, and hot or cold fruit dishes, sherbets, cobblers and crisps. These recipes contain no dairy but rice, soy, goat or homemade seed or nut milks. There is no sugar but it is replaced with Chicolin™/stevia mix. Safe and all natural. The flour I use is light organic spelt.

Bon Appetite and God bless~

Fruit Crisp

1 cup each of raspberries + strawberries (frozen or fresh)
1 apple + 1 large pear (peeled and sliced)
2 cups blueberries (frozen or fresh)
2 tsp. fresh organic lemon juice
1 cup spelt flakes **or** rice flakes
2 Tbsp. light organic spelt flour **or** buckwheat flour
½ tsp. apple pie spice
1½ tsp. Chicolin®/stevia
3 Tbsp Better Butter **or** 2 Tbsp. coconut oil

Preheat oven to 350°. Place all the fruit in a buttered square 9x9-glass pan. Sprinkle the lemon juice over it. Mix the spelt flakes, flour, spice, chicolin mix and butter or oil.

Cover the fruit and bake 30 to 35 minutes. Good with Rice Dream Ice Cream.

Tapioca Pudding

2½ cups favorite milk (soy, rice, nut or goat)
1 Tbsp. Chicolin®/stevia mix
Pinch of sea salt
1 Tbsp. minute tapioca
1 tsp. vanilla extract

Blend milk, chicolin mix, and salt until smooth. Add tapioca let set 5 min. Cook over medium heat until it comes to a boil. It will thicken as it cools. Stir in 1-tsp. vanilla. Serve cold.

Frozen Cherries Jubilee

1 cup Concord grape juice
4½ level Tbsp. Chicolin®/stevia mix
3 oz slivered organic lemon peel
4 Tbsp. starch
5 cups sweet-pitted cherries
2 tsp. brandy extract

Boil juice, chicolin mix, peel to a boil for 4-min. Add cherries. Bring to a boil and simmer 5 min. until cherries are soft. Combine starch and extract together to form a paste. Stir in cherry syrup. Boil 3 min. Add lemon juice and cherries. Ladle into freezer containers and freeze. Heat some into a double boiler to serve over ice cream. Pear and Raspberry Melba Crisp

Bottom layer:

2 heaping Tbsp. Chicolin®/stevia mix
2 Tbsp. organic light spelt flour or tapioca
2 tsp. fresh organic lemon juice
1 tsp. grated lemon rind
½ tsp. cinnamon
3 cups ripe sliced peeled pears
2½ cups blueberries

Preheat oven to 350°. Combine all ingredients. Spread out in 9X9 square pan. Set aside.

Topping:

2/3 cup spelt flakes **or** rice flakes
1/3 cup spelt flour
1½ tsp. Chicolin ®/stevia mix
½ tsp. vanilla extract
2 Tbsp. Better Butter **or** coconut oil

Combine all ingredients. Cover bottom layer. Bake 30 to 35 minutes until brown and fruit is soft. Serve warm with homemade ice cream.

Delicious Old Fashion Rice Pudding

1 cup cooked rice
2 cups favorite milk
2 free range eggs separated
1½ Tbsp. Chicolin®/stevia mix
¼ tsp. sea salt
½ tsp. vanilla extract
1 cup raisins, dates **or** berries

Preheat oven to 350°. In a double boiler, combine rice and milk. Heat to a scalding temperature. In a separate bowl, whip yolks and chicolin mix. Slowly add the hot rice/milk to egg mixture. Continue to whip. Add salt and vanilla. Pour back into saucepan and cook until thick. Add fruit. Pour into a greased casserole. Bake 20 – 25 minutes or until brown.

Trifle

Stale cake (left over)
Berry jam (from your pantry)
Fruit of choice such as peaches, pears, cherries, bananas, blueberries, strawberries or raspberries.
1 beaten range free egg **or** 3 Tbsp. Flax Gel
1 cup of favorite milk such as rice, soy, nut or goat
½ tsp. Chicolin®/stevia mix
1/8 tsp. sea salt

Take egg or flax gel, chicolin mix, salt and cook over hot water until creamy and thick. Set aside. Make your favorite cream sauce or custard. Slice cake in small pieces.

Line in a bowl with cake, spread sauce or custard over cake then spread jam; layer each section and repeat this process until your bowl is filled to the top. Pour sauce or custard on top and add fruit for last layer. Great way to use up left over cake!

Graham Wafers

½ cup each grounded sesame seeds + spelt flakes (grind)
2 cups white organic spelt flour
½ Tbsp. Chicolin®/stevia mix
¼ tsp. sea salt
½ tsp. soda
1/3 cup Better Butter
3 Tbsp. blackstrap molasses
¾ cup favorite milk

Preheat oven 375°. Mix the first 6 dry ingredients together. Cut in the butter until it looks like oatmeal-adding molasses then add the milk. Roll dough until it is paper-thin. Cut into strips. Bake on cookie sheet 10 minutes. This is good when crushed for Flapper pie or any graham pie shell. (3 cups crushed, 1½ Tbsp. chicolin mix, ¼ cup melted Better Butter and ½ tsp. cinnamon). Fill pie shell. Set aside some for topping. Nice with tea.

Flapper Pie

2½ Tbsp. Chicolin®/stevia mix
9 Tbsp. spelt flour **or** starch
3 cups favorite milk
2 free range eggs, separated
1 Tbsp. Better Butter
1 tsp. vanilla extract

In a double boiler or over hot water, cook & stir chicolin mix, flour, & milk until thick. Add the yolks; cook 5 mins; add butter & vanilla. Fill uncooked Graham Wafer pie shell. Beat egg whites + ½ tsp. Chicolin mix, 1/8 tsp. cream of tartar until stiff. Cover pie then add the rest of the crumbs. Brown in 350° oven. Cool.

In Conclusion

Darlton Moore, CH CC, writes in his newsletter that *Candida* is a *"NUISANCE or NIGHTMARE"*. He quotes, "If I should ever (Heaven forbid) get out of control (with the yeast) I would use a combination of diet and natural products that have been effective at killing it off in the entire digestive tract. I would add some specific supplements that trigger my immune system to seek out and destroy the yeast that I know could cause devastation. My personal program would start by buying several cookbooks with diet for Candida sufferers. By buying several books it would allow me to choose a diet I could be comfortable with…"

With this in mind, I will close by advising you to see a professional to be diagnosed and treated. These recipes are only a help to make things easier for you as you are treated. This applies to allergies as well as other food difficulties.

It has been my pleasure to share with you and if you are interested in any of the Collections mentioned in this Collection of information, I can be reached at:

(250) 549-1701

2p's Health Kitchen

3012 29th Street

Vernon, BC CANADA

V1T 5A7 (Zip Code)

May God Bless You Richly,

Jeannine '2P' Edwards

2P's Treasures Cook Book

No Sugar, No Dairy, Made with Spelt
For Allergies, Candida & Diabetes

Enjoy these Recipes!

For All Your Dietary Needs

Now you can eat the foods you LOVE!

May God Bless You Richly,

Jeannine '2P' Edwards

INDEX

Printed in the United States
73611LV00001B